Alice Walker

Twayne's United States Authors Series

Frank Day, Editor

Clemson University

TUSAS 596

Alice Walker
© *1990, Kim Komenich*

Alice Walker

Donna Haisty Winchell

Clemson University

Twayne Publishers • New York
Maxwell Macmillan Canada • Toronto
Maxwell Macmillan International • New York   Oxford   Singapore   Sydney

Alice Walker
Donna Haisty Winchell

Twayne Publishers
Macmillan Publishing Company
866 Third Avenue
New York, New York 10022

Maxwell Macmillan Canada Inc.
1200 Eglinton Avenue East
Suite 200
Don Mills, Ontario M3C 3N1

10 9 8 7 6 5 4 3 2

The paper used in this publication meets the minimum requirements of American National Standard for Information Sciences—Permanence of Paper for Printed Library Materials, ANSI Z39.48-1984. ∞™

Printed and bound in the United States of America.

Library of Congress Cataloging-in-Publication Data

Winchell, Donna Haisty.
    Alice Walker / Donna Haisty Winchell.
        p.   cm. -— (Twayne's United States authors series ; TUSAS 596)
    Includes bibliographical references and index.
    ISBN 0-8057-7642-7
    1. Walker, Alice, 1944–   —Criticism and interpretation. 2. Afro-Americans in literature. I. Title. II. Series.
    PS3573.A425Z94   1992
    813'.54—dc20   91-45309
                                                                            CIP

For my husband, Mark

Contents

Preface

Blinded in one eye at age eight by a careless shot from a brother's BB gun, Alice Walker felt her pretty, vivacious childhood self withdraw and disappear behind a scar that loomed larger in her imagination than it did in actuality. Feeling ugly and outcast, the young Walker escaped into a world of words, reading Shakespeare and the Russian novelists and beginning to write poetry. This isolated little girl became the suicidal young woman who searched unsuccessfully—first at Spelman, a prestigious black women's college, and then at Sarah Lawrence, a prestigious white women's college—for literary models that would link her words to those of women who preceded her.

Walker has acknowledged that her earliest published poems were her means of celebrating with the world the fact that, pushed to the brink of suicide during her senior year at Sarah Lawrence by an unwanted pregnancy, she chose survival. The four novels, two collections of short stories, two collections of essays, and four collections of poems following those first poems represent her celebration of black women who have had the wherewithal to discover inside them selves from which to draw strength, and have thus survived whole, as Walker herself has done.

Fortunately, Walker has written candidly and often about her life and her art. In chapters 1 and 2 I have drawn primarily from her first collection of poems, *Once: Poems,* and from her first collection of essays, *In Search of Our Mothers' Gardens,* to reconstruct Walker's personal and triumphant struggle for survival.

Some of Walker's fictional women, especially her early ones, have not found their inner sources of strength and thus prove too willing to let others determine their definitions of self. They deny themselves out of misplaced loyalty to black men or adherence to societal codes that dictate confining gender roles. In discussing Walker's novels and short stories in chapters 3–7 and in chapter 9, I have tried to show that her female characters grow as they progress from positions of vulnerability to positions of relative strength.

What has too long been neglected in Walker scholarship, especially since the release of the movie version of *The Color Purple,* is the fact that her male characters also grow and change. Men in Walker's fic-

tional world—as in her life—mellow as they age, becoming less threatening sexually. They also assume an androgynous blend of the best of
both male and female characteristics. Walker's male characters achieve
psychological health and wholeness only when they are able to acknowledge women's pain and their role in it. Her women achieve psychological wholeness when they are able to fight oppression, whether
its source is white racism, their own black men, or their own self-
righteous anger. Walker's overwhelming concern is with the survival,
whole, of a people. Although I analyze Walker's two essay collections
in depth in chapters 2 and 8, throughout the discussion of her fiction
I also draw on her nonfiction prose whenever it sheds lights on these
major themes.

Much of Walker's own pain ended at age 27 when she rediscovered,
with the help of her young daughter Rebecca, the beautiful, young,
free self she thought had disappeared forever with her childhood injury.
When Rebecca noticed for the first time the bluish scar in her mother's
eye and saw it not as a defect but as a "world," Walker realized how
much of life is a matter of perspective. Survival whole means in part
choosing which self to celebrate. Part of the celebration of the self in
Walker's work is her characters' acknowledgment that there is something of the divine in everyone and everything in the universe.

Walker herself has mellowed with age. The angry young activist of
the 1960s has become the middle-aged flower child of the 1990s. Her
angry self is now submerged beneath a peaceful exterior. The anger is
there, just below the surface, and it bubbles forth, as it always did, in
response to discrimination, but also increasingly in response to the
greed and destruction that threaten, in the name of progress, the planet
she has known and loved. Her anger during the years blacks were denied the right to coexist in peace and dignity with whites has allied
her with people of all colors who share her belief that the right to
peaceful coexistence should also extend to animals, trees, and all human and nonhuman inhabitants of the earth.

Walker wrote in her journal in January 1984, "Next month I will
be forty. In some ways, I feel my early life's work is done, and done
completely. The books that I have produced already carry forward the
thoughts that I feel the ancestors were trying to help me pass on. In
every generation someone (or two or three) is chosen for this work. . . .
Great Spirit, I thank you for the length of my days and the fullness of
my work. If you wanted me to move on, come home, or whatever is
next, I would try to bear it joyfully."[1] The year before writing this

entry, Walker had won both the Pulitzer Prize and the American Book Award for *The Color Purple*. Whatever "Great Spirit" with which Walker communes must have decided that if her early life's work was done, the entirety of her life's work was not. She went on to publish in 1984 another collection of poems, *Horses Make a Landscape Look More Beautiful*; in 1988 her second collection of essays, *Living by the Word*, discussed in chapter 8; in 1989 her fourth novel, *The Temple of My Familiar*, discussed in chapter 9; and in 1991 *Her Blue Body Everything We Know: Earthling Poems 1965–1990 Complete*.

Toni Morrison once said that she wrote the types of books she wanted to read. Walker responded that she herself wrote rather the types of books that she should have been allowed to read. Walker should take pride in the fact that, with her life's work still unfinished, she has already become for younger artists the model that she was long denied.

Acknowledgments

I am pleased to acknowledge those who have helped in the preparation of this book. I wish to thank Liz Traynor Fowler and Frank Day for their editorial assistance and Susan Ledbetter for her assistance in preparing the index. I also wish to thank Kim Komenich for permission to use his photograph of Ms. Walker. Finally, I would like to thank my husband, Mark, for getting me involved in this project in the first place and for offering me his advice and moral support throughout its completion.

Chronology

1944	Alice Walker born in Eatonton, Georgia, 9 February.
1948	Enters first grade at age four.
1952	Loses sight in her right eye after being shot accidentally with a BB gun by one of her brothers.
1961	Enters Spelman College in Atlanta.
1963	Attends World Youth Peace Festival in Helsinki.
1964–1965	Travels to Africa. Enters Sarah Lawrence College. On the verge of suicide, aborts a pregnancy. Writes her first published short story, "To Hell with Dying," and her first collection of poetry, *Once: Poems*.
1965	Returns during the summer to canvass voters in Liberty County, Georgia. Graduates from Sarah Lawrence.
1966	Spends summer working for the civil rights movement in Mississippi.
1966–1967	Spends winter living with future husband Mel Leventhal in New York. Writes "The Civil Rights Movement: What Good Was It?," which wins first prize in the *American Scholar* essay contest.
1967	Marries Mel Leventhal on 17 March and moves with him to Mississippi, where he is a civil rights attorney in the Jackson school desegregation cases.
1967–1973	Works with Head Start programs and serves as writer in residence at Tougaloo College and Jackson State University.
1968	Attends funeral of Martin Luther King, Jr., and a week later miscarries. *Once: Poems*.
1969	Daughter Rebecca born.
1970	At work on short story "The Revenge of Hannah Kemhuff," discovers the works of Zora Neale Hurston. *The Third Life of Grange Copeland*.

1972   Leaves Mississippi to accept temporary teaching positions at Wellesley College and the University of Massachusetts–Boston.

1973   Father dies. Visits Hurston's grave in Florida. *Revolutionary Petunias* and *In Love and Trouble.*

1974   Moves with Leventhal back to New York and begins work as a contributing editor of *Ms. Langston Hughes: American Poet.*

1976   Divorces Leventhal. *Meridian.*

1977   Receives Guggenheim Memorial Foundation Award.

1978   Moves to San Francisco.

1979   *Good Night, Willie Lee, I'll See You in the Morning* and *I Love Myself When I Am Laughing,* a Zora Neale Hurston reader.

1981   *You Can't Keep a Good Woman Down.*

1982   *The Color Purple.*

1983   Receives Pulitzer Prize and the American Book Award for *The Color Purple. In Search of Our Mothers' Gardens.*

1984   Receives Townsend Prize for *The Color Purple.* Establishes, with Robert Allen, Wild Trees Press. *Horses Make a Landscape Look More Beautiful.*

1988   *Living by the Word* and *To Hell with Dying.*

1989   *Temple of My Familiar.*

1991   *Her Blue Body Everything We Know: Earthling Poems 1965–1990 Complete.*

Chapter One
Survival, Literal and Literary

In 1973 Alice Walker wrote, "Critics seem unusually ill-equipped to discuss and analyze the works of black women intelligently. Generally, they do not even make the attempt; they prefer, rather, to talk about the lives of black women writers, not about what they write."[1] When she wrote those words, Walker was thinking primarily of Zora Neale Hurston, one of the geniuses that America "threw away" in spite of the fact that Hurston's 1937 novel, *Their Eyes Were Watching God,* is, according to Walker and an increasing number of admirers, the healthiest expression of love between a black man and a black woman yet to come out of America.

According to Walker, critics generally disapproved of Hurston not because of her literary style but because of her lifestyle. They disliked her sensuality, her open enjoyment of men whether she married them or not, yet hinted that she must be either gay or bisexual to have such drive. To the critics, she seemed to get Guggenheims and Rosenwalds from white folks much too easily yet remained indifferent to others' opinions of her. Walker concludes, "Although almost everyone agreed she was a delight, not everyone agreed such audacious black delight was permissible, or, indeed, quite the proper image for the race" (*Gardens,* 88–89).

When Walker's first novel, *The Third Life of Grange Copeland,*[2] was published in 1970, she had to deal with the same sort of critical questioning of her "image":

A leading black monthly admitted (the editor did) that the book itself was never read; but the magazine ran an item stating that a *white* reviewer had praised the book (which was, in itself, an indication that the book was no good—so went the logic) and then hinted that the reviewer had liked my book because of my lifestyle. When I wrote to the editor to complain, he wrote me a small sermon on the importance of my "image," of what is "good" for others to see. Needless to say, what others "see" of me is the least of my worries, and I assume that "others" are intelligent enough to recover from whatever shocks my presence or life choices might cause. (*Gardens,* 262)

To the extent that Walker writes about her life choices, the line between her life and her art blurs. To the extent that those life choices—particularly her decision to marry a white man—have the power to shock, she risks having them draw attention from her art. As a young writer Walker read the criticism aimed at Hurston and had to decide if she dared to be herself as fully as Hurston had, risking the same critical disapprobation: "Zora was a woman who wrote and spoke her mind—as far as one could tell, practically always. People who knew her and were unaccustomed to this characteristic in a woman, . . . attacked her as meanly as they could. Would I also be attacked if I wrote and spoke my mind? And if I dared open my mouth to speak, must I always be 'correct'? And by whose standards?" (*Gardens*, 87).

Fortunately, Walker decided to speak her mind, "incorrect" or not. In her fiction and poetry she speaks out by creating characters who are incorrect enough to refuse to be measured by others' standards. In her essays she comments on everything from lesbianism to nuclear weapons, from communism to hairstyles, always including her opinions of the standards by which women in general and women artists in particular are measured. Her autobiographical essays—and all of them are to some degree autobiographical—trace her own developing insights into the social and political forces that have threatened her art, and that of generations of women artists; indeed, they reveal the surprising extent to which Walker's survival as an artist has been bound up with physical survival.

Seeds of Possibility

Part of Walker's understanding of herself as woman and as artist comes from her awareness that she is linked across continents and through generations with women who have exercised their creativity despite the racism and sexism that would deny its expression. In *In Search of Our Mothers' Gardens* (1983), she wrote, "To be an artist and a black woman, even today, lowers our status in many respects, rather than raises it: and yet, artists we will be" (*Gardens*, 237). Walker's art thus far includes four novels, two essay collections, five poetry books, and two short-story collections.

In the essay "In Search of Our Mothers' Gardens," she questions with awed respect how her female ancestors kept alive their creativity during times when even teaching a black man or woman how to read and write was illegal. She writes of mothers and grandmothers who were "driven to a numb and bleeding madness by the springs of creativity in them for which there was no release. . . . Creators, who lived lives of spiritual waste, because they were so rich in spirituality—which is the basis of Art—that the strain of enduring their unused and unwanted talent drove them insane" (*Gardens*, 233). Like the anonymous black woman whose quilt of extraordinary beauty hangs in the Smithsonian Institution, these women expressed their creativity through whatever meager materials society allowed them and "waited for a day when the unknown thing that was in them would be made known; but guessed, somehow in their darkness, that on the day of their revelation they would be long dead" (*Gardens*, 233). Walker mourns the gifts that were stifled within the artists of the past, but her essay goes on to celebrate the future. Many a sculptor, singer, poet, and painter may have died unknown, but the possibility of art did not die. Rather, in the absence of material goods, it became a legacy passed down from mother to daughter: "And so our mothers and grandmothers have, more often than not anonymously, handed on the creative spark, the seed of the flower they themselves never hoped to see: or like a sealed letter they could not plainly read" (*Gardens*, 240).

"In Search of Our Mothers' Gardens" records Walker's discovery of her mother's art form. In the essay Walker draws her imagery from the impressive garden that was her mother's particular means of keeping the creative seed alive wherever the Walkers went as they lived the unsettled life of the Georgia sharecropper. Little in Minnie Tallulah (Lou) Walker's background prepared her for the life of an artist. Minnie Lou ran away from home to marry at 17 and by 20 had two children and another on the way. When Alice was born in Eatonton, Georgia, on 9 February 1944—the first time her parents were able to pay the midwife cash rather than making the usual payment, a pig[3]—she was eighth, last, and unplanned.

Walker's mother's family had lived in Georgia so long that no one remembered how or when they first came there. Walker does know, however, that her father's great-great-grandmother, Mrs. Mary Poole, came as a slave on foot from Virginia, carrying a baby on each hip, a trek that Walker commemorates by keeping her maiden name. Walker points out that, having buried generations of family in the red clay of central Georgia, surely a portion was theirs, yet even the land her father's grandfather managed to buy after the Civil War was taken from him following Reconstruction (*Gardens*, 142–43).

There is no sentimentality in Walker's recollections of Southern country life: "I can recall that I hated it, generally. The hard work in the fields, the shabby houses, the evil greedy men who worked my father to death and almost broke the courage of that strong woman, my mother" (*Gardens*, 21).

Her mother refused to be broken, though, and came home from the fields each day to plant and prune more than 50 different varieties of plants. She covered the holes in the walls of their run-down sharecroppers' cabins with flowers. Walker writes, "Because of her creativity with her flowers, even my memories of poverty are seen through a screen of blooms—sunflowers, petunias, roses, dahlias, forsythia, spirea, delphiniums, verbena . . . and on and on" (*Gardens*, 241). In her garden Mrs. Walker is an artist at work: "I notice that it is only when my mother is working in her flowers that she is radiant, almost to the point of being invisible—except as Creator: hand and eye. She is involved in work her soul must have. Ordering the universe in the image of her personal conception of Beauty. Her face, as she prepares the Art that is her gift, is a legacy of respect she leaves to me, for all that illuminates and cherishes life. She handed down respect for the possibilities—and the will to grasp them" (*Gardens*, 241–42).

Minnie Lou Walker knew that possibility was, in part, tied to education. On behalf of her eight children, she fought for the education she knew was essential if they were ever to escape the sharecropping system, the vicious cycle that kept many a black family perpetually in debt and perpetually on the move. Walker saw her mother's quick, violent temper "only a few times a year, when she battled with the white landlord who had the misfortune to suggest that her children did not need to go to school" (*Gardens*, 238). In the essay, Walker pays tribute to her mother and others of her generation.

At a time when there was not even a high school in Eatonton, one of Walker's sisters, described as "a brilliant, studious girl," became "one of those Negro wonders—who collected scholarships like trading stamps and wandered all over the world" (*Gardens*, 269). Walker herself started school at four when her mother could no longer take her to the fields, and she went on to become her high school's valedictorian.

An accident when Alice was eight, however, helped determine the form her artistic flowering would take. Up to that time Alice had been a precocious child, giving Easter speeches in starched dresses and patent leather shoes and smugly declaring at two and a half, "I'm the prettiest." As she writes, *"It was great fun being cute. But then, one day, it ended" (Gardens,* 386). Her self-confidence ended when she and two of her older brothers were playing cowboys and Indians. A shot from a brother's BB gun injured her right eye leaving it blind and scarred. After the accident she lowered her eyes from the curious stares of others, and for six years she did not raise her head.

From the time of the accident, she writes in "From an Interview," she "daydreamed—not of fairy tales—but of falling on swords, of putting guns to my heart or head, or of slashing my wrists with a razor" (*Gardens,* 244). She felt ugly and disfigured. Out of her isolation, however, grew her art: "I believe . . . that it was from this period—from my solitary, lonely position, the position of an outcast—that I began really to see people and things, really to notice relationships and to learn to be patient enough to care about how they turned out. I no longer felt like the little girl I was. I felt old, and because I felt I was unpleasant to look at, filled with shame. I retreated into solitude, and read stories and began to write poems" (*Gardens,* 244–45).[4]

Mrs. Walker had the wisdom to recognize that Alice had a special gift more valuable than physical beauty. As Mary Helen Washington explains in "Alice Walker: Her Mother's Gifts," a 1982 article based on an interview with Walker, Walker's mother granted her "permission" to be a writer; someone less perceptive might have deemed a sharecropper's cabin in Georgia an odd place to raise a poet.[5] Even when Mrs. Walker was working in the fields or in white women's kitchens and Alice was the only daughter still living at home, Mrs. Walker excused Alice from household chores, respecting her right—and her need—to sit and read.

Washington discusses three gifts Walker's mother bought on layaway out of less than $20 a week she made as a domestic. The first, when her daughter was 15 or 16, was a sewing machine so that Walker could make her own clothes, and as Walker explains, "The message about independence and self-sufficiency was clear." The second was a suitcase, "as nice a one as anyone in Eatonton had ever had. That suitcase gave me permission to travel and part of the joy in going very far from home was the message of that suitcase." The third was a typewriter. "If that wasn't saying, 'Go write your ass off,' I don't know what you need" (Washington, 38).

When Walker was offered a scholarship to Spelman College in Atlanta, the ladies of the Methodist church collected $75 to bless her on her way.

Harvest of Despair

Walker's father, however, feared the world into which they sent his daughter. For Willie Lee Walker education was something to be feared because of the barrier it placed between him and his children. "And why not?" Walker asks. "Though he risked his life and livelihood to vote more than once, nothing changed in his world. Cotton prices continued low. Dairying was hard. White men and women continued to run things, badly. In his whole life my father never had a vacation. . . . Education merely seemed to make his children more critical of him" (*Living,* 13). Walker's experiences at Spelman and then later at Sarah Lawrence in New York, to which she transferred after two and a half years, seem to have confirmed his fears. In "My Father's Country Is the Poor," Walker writes of how her "always tenuous" relationship with her father virtually ended when she left for Spelman: "This brilliant man—great at mathematics, unbeatable at storytelling, but unschooled beyond the primary grades—found the manners of his suddenly middle-class (by virtue of being in college) daughter a barrier to easy contact, if not actually frightening. I found it painful to expose my thoughts in language that to him obscured more than it revealed" (*Gardens,* 216).

It is a commonplace of Walker criticism that she is more sympathetic toward her black male characters as they grow older. Her images of young black male brutality toward women are not surprising; violence was a fact of life in Eatonton in general and in her own family in particular. In an interview with David Bradley, Walker recalls, "I knew both my grandfathers, and they were just doting, indulgent, sweet old men. I just loved them both and they were crazy about me. However, as young men, middle-aged men, they were . . . brutal. One grandfather knocked my grandmother out of a window. He beat one of his children so severely that the child had epilepsy. Just a horrible, horrible man. But when I knew him, he was a sensitive, wonderful man."[6] Asked if her father would have eventually been like her grandfather, Walker replies wistfully, "Oh, he had it in him to be." Unfortunately, although Walker and her father never discussed her works, she feels that as he grew older he became more like some of her worst characters (*Living,* 11). She never saw him mellow into the benevolent old man each of her grandfathers had become.

In the afterword to the 1988 edition of *The Third Life of Grange Copeland,* her fictional portrayal of domestic brutality, she writes, "In my immediate family too there was violence. Its roots seemed always to be embedded in my father's need to dominate my mother and their children and in her resistance (and ours), verbal and physical, to any such domination."[7] In Alice's eyes, his sexist attitudes made him a failure as the male role model he should have been. When his middle daughter, Ruth, showed an interest in boys, he beat her and locked her in her room; he told her never to come home if she found herself pregnant. At the same time, he expected his sons to experiment with sex. Also failures as role models were the four of Walker's five brothers still living at home during the years Walker was old enough to remember: "I desperately needed my father and brothers to give me male models I could respect, because white men (for example; being particularly handy in this sort of comparison)—whether in films or in person—offered man as dominator, as killer, and always as hypocrite. My father failed because he copied the hypocrisy. And my brothers—except for one—never understood they must represent half the world to me, as I must represent the other half to them" (*Gardens,* 330–31).

As Walker herself grew older, she came to understand more fully what made her father what he was. Looking back during the course of a May 1989 *Life* interview with Gregory Jaynes, Walker explains that when her father was 11, his mother was murdered on the way home from church "by a man whose advances she had spurned" and that he "was just crazed by this early pain."[8] Because her sister Ruth resembled his dead mother, "he rejected her and missed no opportunity that I ever saw to put her down" (*Living,* 14).

In "Brothers and Sisters" Walker explains that she understood and forgave her father only when she studied women's liberation ideology. From it she learned that his sexism was merely an imitation of the society in which he lived (*Gardens,* 330). Willie Lee Walker never had the chance for escape that his youngest daughter had. Analyzing her relationship with her father in the 1984 essay "Father," she expresses her love for what he might have been but adds, "Knowing now, at forty, what it takes out of body and spirit to go and how much more to stay, and having learned, too, by now, some of the pitiful confusions in behavior caused by ignorance and pain, I love you no less for what you were" (*Living,* 17). In "My Father's Country Is the Poor," she looks back on the day she boarded the bus for Spelman, leaving him standing beside the lonely Georgia highway. She writes, "I moved—blinded by tears of guilt and relief—ever farther and farther away; until, by the time of his death, all I understood, *truly,* of my father's life, was how

few of its possibilities he had realized, how relatively little of its possible grandeur I had known" (*Gardens,* 216). Walker feels she has
achieved reconciliation with her father only since his death.

One of Walker's most successful stories, "A Sudden Trip Home in
the Spring," is a fictional portrayal of a young black woman's response
to the death of her father. The character, Sarah Davis, feels as alienated
from her father as Walker felt from hers.[9] Word of her father's death
back home in Georgia reaches Sarah at her prestigious girls' school in
New York. One of only two black girls at Cresselton, she is studying
art on a scholarship. (There were six black students at Sarah Lawrence
when Walker was enrolled.) As far as her art is concerned, Sarah faces
two problems: At Cresselton, she lives in a world where there are no
faces like her own, save one, to serve as her models. She also finds
herself incapable of drawing or painting black men because she cannot
"bear to trace defeat onto blank pages" (*GW,* 126).

Like Walker, Sarah feels that she and her father have stopped speaking the same language. She blames him for her mother's death; he
protests that constantly following the crops, moving from one ram-
shackle shack to another, killed her. He, like Walker's father, had his
violent moments. After his death, Sarah wonders, "Did it matter now
that often he had threatened their lives with the rage of his despair?
That once he had spanked the crying baby violently, who later died of
something else altogether . . . and that the next day they moved? She
answers, No . . . I don't think it does" (*GW,* 132). She can say so,
however, only after her trip south for the funeral.

Sarah draws on her reading about black novelist Richard Wright's
experiences with his father to try to decide for herself what a child owes
a father after his death. One of her classmates at Cresselton tells her
that a strong man does not need a father. The implication is that neither does a strong woman. Sarah realizes, however, that her father is
her link to generations of her family, that he is, as Sarah puts it, "one
faulty door in a house of many ancient rooms. Was that one faulty door
to shut [her] off forever from the rest of the house?" (*GW,* 129).

At her father's funeral, Sarah realizes she has seen defeat in black
men's faces only because she has always seen them against a background
of white. Standing at her father's grave, looking at her grandfather out
of the corner of her eye, Sarah thinks, *It is strange . . . that I never
thought to paint him like this, simply as he stands; without anonymous mean-
ingless people hovering beyond his profile; his face turned brownly against the
light.* The defeat that had frightened her in the faces of black men was

the defeat of black forever defined by white" (*GW*, 135). At her father's grave Sarah discovers where one's definition of self should come from: "But that defeat was nowhere on her grandfather's face. He stood like a rock, outwardly calm, the comfort and support of the Davis family. The family alone defined him, and he was not about to let them down" (*GW*, 135). When Sarah realizes she can indeed capture such strength on canvas, her grandfather tells her to capture him in stone instead. Sarah knows finally that in pursuing her art she will be saying "NO with capital letters" to the system that killed her mother and broke her father's spirit.

Sarah finds the "doors" to the house of her heritage in her grandfather and in her brother. If in Walker's own life there is a counterpart to the brother who wraps Sarah in his arms and encourages her to get the education her parents would have wanted for her, it is her oldest brother, Fred, who left home to live and work on his own when Walker was still quite small. (In "Brothers and Sisters" she calls him Jason.) Not until their father's funeral did she meet this older brother again.

In "A Sudden Trip," Sarah and her grandfather are the only ones who do not shed a tear at Sarah's father's funeral. At Willie Lee Walker's, Fred and Alice alone were dry-eyed. Leaving the grave, Fred introduced himself, taking her in his arms and saying, "You don't ever have to walk alone." Walker thought in response, "One out of five ain't *too* bad" (*Gardens,* 330).

When Suicide Is Not Enuf

During her senior year at Sarah Lawrence, Walker's childhood dreams of suicide very nearly became a reality. In "From an Interview" she acknowledges how close she came to death after she returned from a summer trip to Africa "healthy and brown, . . . and pregnant" (*Gardens,* 245). Her father had made it clear that none of his daughters was to come home if she ever found herself pregnant; her mother looked upon abortion as a sin. When Walker reached out to her two sisters, one never replied and the other called her a slut. Feeling at the mercy of everything, including her own body, she slept for three nights with a razor blade under her pillow. At the last moment a friend saved her life by giving her the phone number of an abortionist.

This confrontation with suicide and abortion, together with the isolation she experienced after her childhood eye injury, profoundly influenced Walker. The poems in *Once: Poems,* Walker's first volume of

poetry, were written in an outpouring of creative energy in the week
following her abortion in 1965. She slipped the poems daily under the
cottage door of her teacher and mentor at Sarah Lawrence, Muriel Rukeyser, who passed them along to her editor, who eventually became
Walker's editor at Harcourt, Brace, Jovanovich. *Once* was not published
until 1968, when Walker was 24.[10]

Walker recalls that in *Once*, she wrote her reminiscences about Africa
first "because the vitality and color and friendships in Africa rushed
over me in dreams the first night I slept" (*Gardens*, 248). In some
stanzas of the African poems the influence of William Carlos Williams's
imagism, Zen epigrams, and Japanese haiku is evident. Elsewhere, the
fact that these are apprenticeship works is evidenced by her tendency
to use punctuation rather than images to achieve an effect.

Some of the most poignant passages in *Once* go beyond the "vitality
and color and friendships" to capture a pride on the part of the African
people that refuses to yield to the harsher realities of African life. One
of the proud Karamojans she meets is a noble savage whose naked body
has the classic beauty of a statue but whose eyes are running sores. The
brightness in a little Karamojan girl's eyes merely signals the onset of
glaucoma. Flies swarm around the bare breasts of an old woman of 20.
Of these proud Karamojans, perhaps 100 are left.

Poems in the second section are about another proud people, American blacks at odds with a racist society. In these poems there surface
submerged memories of marches, picketing, Southern jails, and police
brutality from Walker's years in Atlanta. The individuals who populate
the series of vignettes that constitute the long title poem "Once" are
often people whose bold and sometimes audacious behavior would have
made Zora Neale Hurston proud. There is the young black man who
wants to break all barriers at once by swimming nude at a white beach
in Alabama. There is the half-wit charged with indecent exposure because he likes the way his black skin looks when he steps from his
bathtub. And there is the black man, rejected by a bosomy blonde in
a G-string because she does not want to end up with her shapely legs
dangling from a poplar, who points out that hers would look much
prettier dangling there than his would.

The height of audacity is illustrated by a character based on one of
Walker's real-life marching mates, "a beautiful girl who spoke French
and came to Spelman from Tuskegee, Alabama . . . whose sense of
style was unfaltering, in the worst of circumstances" (*Gardens*, 254).
In the poem "Chic Freedom's Reflection" she stands on tiptoe to pow-
der her nose in the badge of a Southern lawman.

The love poems in *Once* clearly demonstrate that even in her early career Walker was seeking a universal love that would cross all boundaries—racial, sexual, geographic, and temporal. The narrator in "The Smell of Lebanon" offers her bosom to an Arab student, and the narrator in "The Black Prince" offers her companionship to a newly arrived village chief so that he will not have to spend his first night in London alone. Like Hurston, Walker was not afraid of being condemned for honestly presenting a sexual freedom that her audience might judge "incorrect." In fact, when she wrote these poems she was not worrying about an audience at all. (She did want someone to read them, and that someone was her mentor, Rukeyser.)

Walker does worry, in retrospect, that two poems in the volume are "dishonest" (*Gardens,* 271). One is "Ballad of the Brown Girl," in which the girl commits suicide because she cannot take a white baby home to her father. Here love fails to cross the racial barrier. In the other, "Johann," Walker imagines the consternation Hitler would have felt in response to a blue-eyed blond man's desire to have bronze children with a brown woman. Walker feels the poem is dishonest because it glosses over a fear of the unfamiliar she herself had not yet been able to overcome.

Walker tells us that the last section of poems, about suicide, grew out of feelings that she experienced during the three days she waited to die. In them death seems a relatively pleasant alternative to despair, a declaration Walker makes in a poem forthrightly entitled "To Die Before One Wakes Must Be Glad." In "Suicide" she sets forth "guidelines" for suicide: that suicide notes should be written, signed in blood, and to the point, even if that point is there is none; that the desire simply to rest should be acknowledged for the laziness that it is; and that those who are outraged should consider if the happy days of their happiest summer number even one. If not, death at least contributes to the ongoing cycle of life, as Walker points out in the first stanza of "Exercises on Themes from Life," where she describes both death and decay as on their way to being daffodils.

A Celebration of Life

With *Once,* Walker made her successful debut as a poet. The volume went almost immediately into a second printing. She explains the effect its appearance had on her: "By the time *Once* was published . . . the book itself did not seem to me important; only the writing of the poems, which clarified for me how very much I loved being alive. . . .

Since that time, it seems to me that all of my poems—and I write groups of poems rather than singles—are written when I have successfully pulled myself out of a completely numbing despair, and stand again in the sunlight. Writing poems is my way of celebrating with the world that I have not committed suicide the evening before" (*Gardens*, 249).

At 21 Walker had learned that writing does, in a quite literal sense, save lives. She also credits an old artist in Georgia with turning her attention to life at a time when death was much on her mind. The death of that friend became the subject of her first published short story, "To Hell with Dying," and the difference in title alone between this and the first one she wrote, "The Suicide of an American Girl," reveals a change in outlook.

"To Hell with Dying" is the fictionalized account of the death of the drunken old guitar player who was Walker's "first love."[11] In response to frequent questions about links between her life and her art, Walker uses this story as an example of an autobiographical work. As she explains, "The *love* happened, and that is the essence of the story" (*Living*, 37).

In the story, each time old Mr. Sweet totters on the brink of death, a neighbor, based on Walker's father, brings all of his children into the room, shoving the doctor aside and shouting, "To hell with dying, man, these children want Mr. Sweet!" and the children kiss and tickle him back to life. This ritual works until Mr. Sweet is 90 and the narrator is at work on her doctorate far away in Massachusetts. She drops everything to fly home, but this time she cannot save him.

Walker was in New York, of course, not in Massachusetts, and she had no money to fly home either to "save" Mr. Sweet or to attend his funeral. When the story was published as a children's book in 1988, [12] Walker wrote "The Old Artist: Notes on Mr. Sweet" to explain how it came about. She wrote,

Turning my back on the razor blade, I went to a friend's house for Christmas holidays (I was too poor even to consider making the trip home, a distance of about a thousand miles), and on the day of Mr. Sweet's burial I wrote "To Hell with Dying." If in my poverty I had no other freedom—not even to say good-bye to him in death—I still had the freedom to love him and the means to express it, if only to myself. I wrote the story with tears pouring down my cheeks, I was grief-stricken, I was crazed, I was fighting for my life. I was twenty-one. (*Living*, 39)

Walker could not save Mr. Sweet, but with his help she did save herself. The story is her wish that she could have returned the favor. Contemplating suicide, she recalled the magnitude of the problems Mr. Sweet had faced in a lifetime in the American South, but also the fact that in spite of those problems, he had continued to sing. Mr. Sweet was awarded a place of respect and honor in the Walker home, despite the fact that he drank and gambled, because he was an artist: "He went deep into his own pain and brought out words and music that made us happy, made us feel empathy for anyone in trouble, made us think. We were taught to be thankful that anyone would assume this risk" (*Living,* 38). It was the same risk that Walker took in choosing to be an artist. As surely as Minnie Lou Walker, Zora Neale Hurston, and generations of women before them kept alive the seed of creativity and passed it on to the next generation, so did Mr. Sweet, a fact critics ignore when they deny the presence of positive male role models in Walker's works. The seed of creativity was Mr. Sweet's legacy to Walker. In the story the gift of creativity is passed on symbolically in the form of Mr. Sweet's guitar.

Muriel Rukeyser sent "To Hell with Dying" to Langston Hughes, who published it two years later in *Best Short Stories by Negro Writers.*[13] Of this "greatest of the old black singer poets," Walker writes, "When I met Langston Hughes I was amazed. He was another Mr. Sweet! Aging and battered, full of pain, but writing poetry, and laughing, too, and always making other people feel better. It was as if my love for one great old man down in the poor and beautiful and simple South had magically, in the new world of college and literature and poets and publishing and New York, led me to another" (*Living,* 40). In 1974 Walker honored Hughes by adding her *Langston Hughes: American Poet* to the Crowell series of biographies for children.[14]

Chapter Two
Survival Whole: *In Search of Our Mothers' Gardens*

In Search of Our Mothers' Gardens (1983), a collection of essays, articles, reviews, and speeches Walker wrote between 1966 and 1982, is subtitled "Womanist Prose." She prefers the term *womanist* to *feminist*, defining a *womanist* as "a feminist of color" and "a woman who loves other women, sexually or nonsexually" yet "is committed to survival and wholeness of entire people, male *and* female" (*Gardens*, xi). Much of the volume analyzes the forces of racism and sexism that deny people wholeness.

Although Walker found publishers for her early works with relative ease, she has been frustrated and angry that during the years she was growing into her art she was largely denied the aid of black literary models. In "Saving the Life That Is Your Own: The Importance of Models in the Artist's Life," Walker characterizes "the absence of models, in literature as in life" as "an occupational hazard for the artist, simply because models in art, in behavior, in growth of spirit and intellect—even if rejected—enrich and enlarge one's view of existence" (*Gardens*, 4).

She eventually found the models she needed, but not at Spelman or at Sarah Lawrence, where she heard "not one word about early black women writers" (*Gardens*, 9). She later discovered that her years at first a prestigious black college and then a prestigious white one had left her with a "blind spot" in her education: "I began to feel that subtly and without intent or malice, I had been miseducated. For where my duty as a black poet, writer, and teacher would take me, people would have little need of Keats and Byron or even Robert Frost, but much need of Hughes, Bontemps, Gwendolyn Brooks, and Margaret Walker" (*Gardens*, 131–32). When Walker told a white Northerner that she planned to be a poet, he hinted that "a 'farmer's daughter' might not be the stuff of which poets are made." She acknowledges that there was perhaps some logic in what he said, but that the "stuff" of the poet's art must be dictated by the audience for which she writes: "A shack with only a dozen or so books is an unlikely place to discover a young Keats. But it is narrow thinking, indeed, to believe that a Keats is the only kind of poet one would want to grow up to be. One wants to write poetry that is understood by one's people, not by the Queen of England" (*Gardens,* 18).

After moving to Mississippi in 1967, she audited a course at Jackson State University taught by the poet Margaret Walker, one of the few black women writers whose works were in print. Ironically, even there the focus was solely on black male writers such as Charles Chesnutt, Jean Toomer, Langston Hughes, Richard Wright, Ralph Ellison, and James Baldwin; black women writers were mentioned, but not read, partly because their works were largely unavailable. When Walker returned to address the student body at Sarah Lawrence in 1972, she noted with regret that some faculty members still felt there was not enough literature of merit by black authors to warrant a year's course. In her address, however, she encouraged each young woman leaving college to seek out those writers not yet granted a place in the canon: "There are countless vanished and forgotten women who are nonetheless eager to speak to her—from Frances Harper and Anne Spencer to Dorothy West—but she must work to find them, to free them from their neglect and the oppression forced upon them because they were black and they were women" (*Gardens,* 36).

She recalls Toni Morrison's answer to why she wrote the books she did. Morrison pointed out that she wrote the sorts of books she wanted to read. Walker adds that she herself writes the sorts of books she should have been able to read (*Gardens,* 13). The course in black women writers she taught in the early 1970s first at Wellesley and later at the University of Massachusetts–Boston was, she believes, the first of its kind.

Walker's anger at being deprived of appropriate models comes out in one of the most famous essays in *In Search of Our Mothers' Gardens,* "Beyond the Peacock: The Reconstruction of Flannery O'Connor." She tells of going with her mother to visit first the sharecroppers' house on the Eatonton–to–Milledgeville road in Georgia where the Walker family lived briefly in 1952, and then, just a few miles down the road, the house where O'Connor lived from 1951 until her death from lupus in 1964. Walker recalls how, at Sarah Lawrence, she had been an avid reader of O'Connor's works until she angrily put them aside when she realized there were other female writers she was not being allowed to read. When Walker sees the contrast between the two empty houses the rage she felt at college resurfaces. Two of the four rooms of her family's house have rotted away; the others are filled with hay. The O'Connor home, Andalusia, is still neatly kept although no one lives there. Walker stands with her mother on the front porch of Andalusia, knocking on a door she knows no one will answer, feeling the anger well up inside her:

What I feel at the moment of knocking is fury that someone is paid to take care of her house, though no one lives in it, and that her house still, in fact, stands, while mine—which of course we never owned anyway—is rotting into dust. Her house becomes—in an instant—the symbol of my own disinheritance, and for that instant I hate her guts. All that she has meant to me is diminished, though her diminishment within me is against my will. . . . Standing there knocking on Flannery O'Connor's door, I do not think of her illness, her magnificent work in spite of it; I think: it all comes back to houses. To how people live. There are rich people who own houses to live in and poor people who do not. And this is wrong. Literary separatism, fashionable now among blacks as it has always been among whites, is easier to practice than to change a fact like this. I think: I would level this country with the sweep of my hand, if I could.
    "Nobody can change the past," says my mother.
    "Which is why revolutions exist," I reply. (*Gardens,* 57–58)

These are not Walker's essays about revolution; they come later in the volume. These are essays about survival, literary and otherwise, and about literary models.

Walker acknowledges that anger is a threat to her psyche, a waste of energy that could better be used in other endeavors—her own art, for example. She leaves the house knowing she will continue to love that in O'Connor's art which is admirable and to "let the rest rot" like the sharecroppers' cabin Walker once called home. One part of the Walker heritage that still flourishes in that Georgia pasture, however, is the flowers Walker's mother nurtured wherever the family lived: her mother's art.

Continuity of Time

When, on their trip to Milledgeville, her mother asked what she was looking for when she made these trips south, Walker replied, "A wholeness." She felt that everything around her was "split up, deliberately split up. History split up, literature split up, and people are split up, too" (*Gardens,* 48). Walker preserved the health of her own spirit despite the anger she felt on O'Connor's doorstep. Her solution to the split between literature by blacks and literature by whites—the fashionable literary separatism she refers to in "Beyond the Peacock"—was to "take what you can use and let the rest rot" (*Gardens,* 59). Walker took a major step toward resolving the problem of historical division, however, when she finally discovered her link with black artists who had gone before her. In "Saving the Life That Is Your Own" Walker argues that "what is always needed in the appreciation of art, or life, is the larger perspective. Connections made, or at least attempted, where none existed before, the straining to encompass in one's glance at the varied world the common thread, the unifying theme through immense diversity" (*Gardens,* 5). One of the most valuable gifts Walker gained in discovering her literary ancestors was a sense of continuity with the past, a thread that bound her to a community of black artisans.

In "The Black Writer and the Southern Experience" Walker explains that the black Southern writer inherits a sense of community and with it the responsibility to speak for that community, to "give voice to centuries not only of silent bitterness and hate but also of neighborly kindness and sustaining love" (*Gardens,* 21). Looking back, Walker appreciates the positive material she draws from her "underprivileged" background.

Her appreciation of that background was enhanced when she discovered Zora Neale Hurston and her efforts to preserve the cultural heritage that the two shared. In late 1970 Walker was at work on a short story based on an incident from her mother's life when she discovered she needed some authentic material on voodoo practiced by blacks in the South in the 1930s. She turned first to the white folklorists but found them, at best, condescending and, at worst, blatantly racist. During her research, however, in a footnote she discovered a reference to Hurston. Walker's initial encounter with Hurston as she worked on the story, "The Revenge of Hannah Kemhuff," had such an impact on her personally and professionally that she has written about it repeatedly—in the essays "Saving the Life That Is Your Own," "The Black Writer and the Southern Experience," "The Unglamorous but Worthwhile Duties of the Black Revolutionary Artist," and elsewhere. Walker deals most directly with Hurston and Hurston's influence on her, however, in "Zora Neale Hurston: A Cautionary Tale and a Partisan View" and in "Looking for Zora."

When Walker left Sarah Lawrence, she entered what she terms a different "college" of musty old books, old black men and women, and the young, "students and dropouts who articulate in various bold and shy ways that they believe themselves to be without a valuable history, without a respectable music, without writing or poetry that speaks to them" (*Gardens*, 132). The book she turned to in 1970, one not so much musty but out of print and hard to find, was Hurston's collection of folklore *Mules and Men*. Walker admits she violated someone's rights by photocopying Hurston's book because it was the only way she could read it again and again. Walker discovered in Hurston a voice speaking to her and to her family across the years:

When I read *Mules and Men* I was delighted. Here was this perfect book! The "perfection" of which I immediately tested on my relatives, who are such typical black Americans they are useful for every sort of political, cultural, or economic survey. Very regular people from the South, rapidly forgetting their Southern cultural heritage in the suburbs and ghettos of Boston and New York, they sat around reading the book themselves, listening to me read the book, listening to each other read the book, and a kind of paradise was regained. For what Zora's book did was this: it gave them back all the stories they had forgotten or of which they had grown ashamed (told to us years ago by our parents and grandparents—not one of whom could *not* tell a story to make you weep, or laugh) and showed how marvelous, and, indeed, priceless, they are. This is not exaggerated. No matter how they read the stories Zora had collected, no matter how much distance they tried to maintain between themselves, as new sophisticates, and the lives their parents and grandparents lived, no matter how they tried to remain cool toward all Zora revealed, in the end they could not hold back the smiles, the laughter, the joy over who she was showing them to be: descendants of an inventive, joyous, courageous, and outrageous people; loving drama, appreciating wit, and, most of all, relishing the pleasure of each other's loquacious and *bodacious* company. (*Gardens*, 84–85)

Here was the model Walker had been searching for. Here was her link between past and present, her means of achieving continuity of time. Having discovered Hurston, Walker was able to link the survival of the artist to the survival of cultural heritage. Hurston had left the South, studied anthropology with Franz Boas at Barnard College in New York, and returned to preserve the oral culture of her people—

the "big old lies," or folklore, of the rural black community. *Mules and Men,* Hurston's record of that culture, gave Walker the background she needed for the short story "The Revenge of Hannah Kemhuff," published in *The Best Short Stories of 1974.* Writing the story profoundly affected Walker:

> I mention it because this story might never have been written, because the very bases of its structure, authentic black folklore, viewed from a black perspective, might have been lost.
>
> Had it been lost, my mother's story would have had no historical underpinning, none I could trust, anyway. I would not have written the story, which I enjoyed writing as much as I've enjoyed writing anything in my life, had I not known that Zora had already done a thorough job of preparing the ground over which I was then moving.
>
> In that story I gathered up the historical and psychological threads of the life my ancestors lived, and in the writing of it I felt joy and strength and my own continuity. I had that wonderful feeling writers get sometimes, not very often, of being *with* a great many people, ancient spirits, all very happy to see me consulting and acknowledging them, and eager to let me know that, indeed, I am not alone. (*Gardens,* 13)

In Hurston, Walker found a kindred spirit with whom she shared a concern for the survival of a people and their culture. She also found what she calls the quality most characteristic of Hurston's work: "racial health; a sense of black people as complete, complex, *undiminished* human beings" (*Gardens,* 85). Thus Hurston, like Walker, was not concerned merely with the survival of her people, but with their survival *whole.* Walker attributes Hurston's confidence in herself, and her pride in black men and women, to the fact that she grew up in the all-black town of Eatonville, Florida.

The tragedy of Zora Neale Hurston is that her genius was not recognized during her lifetime. Hurston died in a Florida welfare home. She had written six books, including *Mules and Men* and the novel *Their Eyes Were Watching God,* of which Walker has said, *"There is no book more important to me than this one"* (*Gardens,* 86). As Hurston provided Walker a critical link to her literary past, Walker feels an obligation as an artist to look to the future. "Zora Neale Hurston" concludes, *"We are a people. A people do not throw their geniuses away.* And if they are thrown away, it is our duty *as artists and as witnesses for the future* to collect them again for the sake of our children, and, if necessary, bone by bone" (*Gardens,* 92). "Looking for Zora" is Walker's account of traveling to Florida to look for Hurston's unmarked grave and to buy a monument for it. In 1979 Walker made Hurston's works more accessible by editing a Hurston reader entitled *I Love Myself When I Am Laughing.*[1]

Walker would agree that we have a duty as artists and witnesses for the future to preserve as well the stories of those unknown men and women whose everyday lives constitute the communal past. The year before Walker discovered Hurston's work, she worked as a consultant for Friends of the Children of Mississippi, teaching black history to teachers in Headstart centers. During two week-long workshops she taught 90 women how to teach "blackness" to small children. From various parts of the state, most of the women were black, with little formal education; some were schoolteachers, but many were maids or fieldworkers.

Among the questions that plagued her were these: "How *do* you teach earnest but educationally crippled middle-aged and older women the significance of their past? How do you get them to understand the pathos and beauty of a heritage they have been taught to regard with shame? . . . How do you show a connection between present and past when, as eloquent but morally befuddled Faulkner wrote, 'the past is not even past'?" (*Gardens*, 28).

She decided to try to teach them their place in the history of the American South by asking each woman to write her own history. Her goal: "that they see themselves and their parents and grandparents as part of a living, working, creating movement in Time and Place" (*Gardens*, 28–29). She records some of those histories in "But Yet and Still the Cotton Gin Kept on Working. . . ." When she wrote the essay, she was still compiling their stories, but she had been fired as a consultant because the Office of Economic Opportunity, which provided most of her salary, frowned on black studies courses as part of the training for Headstart teachers.

Wholly/Holy Women

The other three pieces in part 1 of *In Search of Our Mothers' Gardens* are reviews of works by writers whom Walker looks upon as either literary or life models, or both. Most of the models Walker refers to are women, but Jean Toomer has earned a place on her list.

"The Divided Life of Jean Toomer" is a *New York Times* review of *The Wayward and the Seeking* (1980), a collection of autobiographical fragments, short stories, poems, and plays by Toomer, edited and shaped by Darwin T. Turner. One reason Walker seems drawn to Toomer is that he was "a man who cared what women felt" (*Gardens,* 13). As a "womanist" she is intrigued by what the autobiographical fragments reveal about Toomer's mother, who was never free of her husband's domination, and his grandmother, who, with her "dark blood," was dominated by her husband until his health declined and she "blossomed magnificently" (*Gardens,* 62). As was the case for Walker herself, some of Toomer's "songs" were stories that had come to him from his mother and his grandmother.

Walker regrets the sense of loss some readers must feel learning of Toomer's choice to live his life as a white man. He seems to have deluded himself into believing that he could discard racial labels and live simply as an American, one of a new breed, neither black nor white. In writing about the South, however, Toomer felt he was writing about a dying culture and that *Cane* was its swan song. Where Hurston sought to preserve the culture of the South, Toomer sought to sing it to its rest. Walker is not able to say of Toomer what she said of O'Connor; she may not be willing to "let the rest rot," but she is willing to keep the beauty that is *Cane* and let Toomer go.

"A Writer Because of, Not in Spite of, Her Children" is Walker's review of *Second Class Citizen* by Nigerian novelist Buchi Emecheta, who reminded Walker once more of the connection between the future and the past made possible through art. Walker was attracted to this heavily autobiographical novel because Emecheta seemed to have solved a problem that plagued Walker herself: how to balance the demands of her art and the demands of motherhood. Emecheta managed to write her novels against the "sweet background noises" of five children; Walker felt she heard a baby screaming through everything she wrote for a year after her daughter Rebecca's birth. For Emecheta's main character, Adah, the artist's link with the future is the adults that her children will become, and it is for that audience that Adah writes. Walker adds, "I agree that it is healthier, in any case, to write for the adults one's children will become than for the children one's 'mature' critics often are" (*Gardens,* 69).

"*Gifts of Power*" is a review of a book of the same name by the nineteenth-century preacher and mystic Rebecca Jackson. Walker uses the story of Rebecca Jackson to return to defining "wholeness," the subject that introduced this section of essays. Jackson was born in Philadelphia of free black parents in 1795. At 35 she experienced a spiritual conversion, the first of many communications with the Divine. Later she was able suddenly to read the Bible by means of some mysterious act of divine intervention. Her illiteracy was thus removed but another obstacle to her fulfillment of her calling to preach the word of God remained. Her husband insisted she fulfill her sexual obligations toward him, something she could no longer do. After she left her husband she met a younger woman, Rebecca Perot. Jackson lived and traveled with Perot for the remaining 30-odd years of her life.

Walker praises Jean McMahon Humez for her magnificent editing of *Gifts of Power,* but calls her to task for this statement about Jackson's relationship with Perot: "Perhaps, had she been born in the modern age, she would have been an open lesbian" (*Gardens,* 79). This in spite of Jackson's renunciation of the "sin of the fall." The story of Jackson leads Walker to consider whether the term *lesbian* is ever appropriately applied to black women.

The word *lesbian* may not, in any case, be suitable (or comfortable) for black women, who surely would have begun their woman-bonding earlier than Sappho's residency on the Isle of Lesbos. Indeed, I can imagine black women who love women (sexually or not) hardly thinking of what Greeks were doing; but, instead, referring to themselves as "whole" women, from "wholly" or "holy." Or as "round" women—women who love other women, yes, but women who also have concern, in a culture that oppresses all black people (and this would go back very far), for their fathers, brothers, and sons, no matter how they feel about them as males. (*Gardens,* 81)

Any word chosen by such women to describe themselves "would have to be a word that affirmed connectedness to the entire community and the world, rather than separation, *regardless* of who worked or slept with whom" (*Gardens,* 81). In "Breaking Chains and Encouraging Life," a review of *Conditions: Five. The Black Women's Issues,* a collection of poems, essays, reviews, and journal entries by both lesbians and nonlesbians, Walker expresses her regret that even in the modern age there are still women who are denied a sense of connectedness with the literary community because they love women rather than (or more than) men.

Continuity of Place

Where Walker's focus in part 1 of *In Search of Our Mothers' Gardens* is on a sense of shared community and the art that expresses it, part 2 examines the effects of the civil rights movement of the 1960s on the black community and on her own life.

The essays in part 2 span a decade of the history of the movement and of Walker's own history. The section opens with an essay written in the winter of 1966–1967 while she was living in New York with an Irish Jew from New England, law student Melvyn Leventhal, whom she married in March 1967 (relinquishing a McDowell Colony Fellowship to do so). Together they moved to Mississippi. This opening essay, "The Civil Rights Movement: What Good Was It?," Walker's first published essay, won first prize in the 1967 *American Scholar* essay contest. In the 1976 essay that closes the civil rights section of *Gardens,* "Recording the Seasons," she is still trying to answer the same question—what good was the civil rights movement?—and answering it in terms of her own role as revolutionary artist.

Walker's original answer to the question posed in the title "The Civil Rights Movement: What Good Was It?" is that it gave black people each other—an idea that echoes Hurston's gift to her people—and that it gave them the knowledge of their condition. To those who argue that the movement is dead and to those who ask whether it would have been better to leave black people unawakened and unhopeful, her answer is, "I do not think so. If knowledge of my condition is all the freedom I get from a 'freedom movement,' it is better than unawareness, forgottenness, and hopelessness, the existence of a beast" (*Gardens,* 121).

For Walker herself, knowledge meant broadening horizons: "Just 'knowing' has meant everything to me. Knowing has pushed me out into the world, into college, into places, into people" (*Gardens,* 125). Television images of Martin Luther King, Jr., replaced the actors and actresses of the phony world of white soap operas: "He did not say we had to become carbon copies of the white American middle class; but he did say we had the right to become whatever we wanted to become" (*Gardens,* 125). King gave Walker and countless others the option of leaving home in order to become whatever they wanted to become, but he also made it possible for them to come home again, and the continuity of place that he made possible was one of the lasting fruits of the civil rights movement.

Walker explores this theme of continuity of place, and the sense of community it makes possible, in two essays: "Choice: a Tribute to Dr. Martin Luther King, Jr." and "Choosing to Stay at Home." In these and the other essays in *Gardens* she traces her own journey north and then back south.

In "Choice," Walker recalls watching her seven brothers and sisters leave their home in Georgia one after another and awakening to her own realization that "in order just to continue to love the land of my birth, I was expected to leave it" because "to stay willingly in a beloved but brutal place is to risk losing the love and being forced to acknowledge only the brutality" (*Gardens,* 143). The first time she saw King on television, being handcuffed and shoved into a police truck, however, she knew she would fight to stay home: "At the moment I saw his resistance I knew I would never be able to live in this country without resisting everything that sought to disinherit me, and I would never be forced away from the land of my birth without a fight" (*Gardens,* 144).

The most important thing King did for his people, in Walker's estimation, was to give them back their heritage and their homeland. In "Choosing to Stay Home," she looks back 10 years to the famous 1963 march on Washington. She recalls that she could never regret having heard King's famous speech; she had never heard a black person encourage anyone to "Go back to Mississippi." King's speech that day strengthened her resolve to stay home and to fight for that right if necessary: "We would proceed with the revolution from our own homes" (*Gardens,* 161).

Walker left the South to spend summers during her first years at college with family in Boston, and she went to Sarah Lawrence to finish her education, but in the summer of 1965, after her graduation, she did return to the South—to register voters in Georgia. In 1966, despite plans to go to Africa, she went to Mississippi, where she met Leventhal, an attorney involved in the civil rights movement. She writes, "That summer marked the beginning of a realization that I could never live happily in Africa—or anywhere else—until I could live freely in Mississippi" (*Gardens,* 163). When she and Leventhal moved there in 1967 (he was the prosecutor in the Jackson school desegregation cases), a racially mixed couple could not legally live together, married or not. Walker mentions that for several years they were the only interracial, married, home-owning couple in Mississippi. Writing from Mississippi, however, she could still say that when she did leave the state, it would not be out of fear. Rather, "it will be because the pervasive football culture bores me, and the proliferating Kentucky Fried Chicken stands appall me, and neon lights have begun to replace the trees. It will be because the sea is too far away and there is not a single mountain here. But most of all, it will be because I have freed myself to go; and it will be My Choice" (*Gardens,* 170).

In Mississippi, Walker realized that without continuity of place the consciousness of the emerging artist is threatened. Black artists, like blacks in general, tended to leave the South, a place inhospitable to their art; by departing they left the region further impoverished. There she had to define her own role as an artist in the revolution occurring around her. Walker did not lack material to write about, and she wrote feverishly for two years. Yet at the end of the two years she found herself once again becoming suicidal.

Walker attributes her mental distress during this time in part to her pacifism: "The burden of a nonviolent, pacifist philosophy in a violent, nonpacifist society caused me to feel, almost always, as if I had not done enough. When I was working well and the poems and stories grew, I had no time to think of this. When the writing went badly, I questioned the value of writing at all. It did not seem equal to the goals of many of the people who came to visit us during that time" (*Gardens,* 225–26).

She fantasized about "sneaking into various oppressors' houses perhaps disguised as a maid and dropping unplugged hand grenades in their laps" (*Gardens,* 225). Fortunately, she wrote instead—"writing saved me from the sin and *inconvenience* of violence" (*Gardens,* 369)—and, with the help of a black female psychiatrist, discovered the source of her depression: "I became increasingly aware that I was holding myself responsible for the condition of black people in America. Unable to murder the oppressors, I sat in a book-lined study and wrote about lives that persisted in seeming quite extraordinary to me, whatever their subjects' situations.

"In short, I could see that I felt Art was not enough and that my art, in particular, would probably change nothing. And yet I felt it was the privilege of my life to observe and 'save' for the future some extraordinary lives" (*Gardens,* 226–27).

In addition to feeling the pressure of her role as an artist in time of revolution, Walker was also feeling the pressures of motherhood. During 1968 and early 1969 Walker had been desperately trying to get pregnant so that Leventhal could avoid the draft (*Gardens,* 366–67). A week after she marched in King's funeral procession in April 1968, she suffered a miscarriage. As she and her husband counted the days until he would be 26, thereby avoiding service, she found herself pregnant in March 1969. That November, when Walker was 25, her only child,

Rebecca, was born three days after she finished *The Third Life of Grange Copeland.*

Walker feared the effect that motherhood would have on her art. In *"One* Child of One's Own: A Meaningful Digression Within the Work(s),"* she puts that fear in perspective: "My first mistake was in thinking 'children' instead of 'child.' My second was in seeing The Child as my enemy rather than the racism and sexism of an oppressive capitalist society. My third was in believing none of the benefits of having a child would accrue to my writing" (*Gardens,* 363).

In time she came to acknowledge Rebecca's birth as the gift that it was, "the incomparable gift of seeing the world at quite a different angle than before, and judging it by standards that would apply far beyond my natural life" (*Gardens,* 369). The previously suicidal young mother was able to acknowledge that her daughter's birth and accompanying difficulties produced in her "a depth of commitment to [her] own life hard to comprehend otherwise" (*Gardens,* 369). She realized that in reality motherhood was the least of the obstacles to her writing: "In any case, it is not my child who tells me: I have no femaleness white women must affirm. Not my child who says: I have no rights black men must respect. . . . We are together, my child and I. Mother and child, yes, but *sisters* really, against whatever denies us all that we are" (*Gardens,* 382).

When Walker and her family drove down their street for the last time after seven years in Mississippi, she could not look back. Had the civil rights movement done any good? Were conditions any better than they had been in 1963 when she listened with such hope to King in Washington? In "Choosing to Stay at Home" she admits that "the mountain of despair *has* dwindled, and the stone of hope has size and shape, and can be fondled by the eyes and by the hand." Blacks were returning to the South. Her brothers had bought the land surrounding their mother's birthplace in Georgia (*Gardens,* 167–68). Walker herself could say that 10 years after the march on Washington, she could "walk about Georgia (and Mississippi) eating, sleeping, loving, singing, burying the dead—the way men and women are supposed to do in a place that is the only 'home' they've ever known" (*Gardens,* 255). "But freedom," she wrote in the same year, "has always been an elusive tease, and in the very act of grabbing for it one can become shackled" (*Gardens,* 168). She knew that black women would never be free until their right to that freedom was recognized, as it often had not been, by white women who called themselves feminists and by black men who called themselves brothers, beside whom black women had fought for the cause of civil rights.

Healthy and Whole

While in Mississippi, Walker had taught at Jackson State University and Tougaloo College. During an 18-month escape from Mississippi with her young daughter in 1972–1973, she did some teaching at Wellesley College and at the University of Massachusetts–Boston. When she left Mississippi for good in 1974, she became an editor at *Ms.* and, in 1977, an associate professor of English at Yale University.

Walker's marriage to Leventhal ended in 1978. In that year she moved to San Francisco, where she now lives with Robert Allen, a writer and former member of the board of directors of *Black Scholar* and her partner in Wild Trees Press. She had known Allen at Spelman College in the 1960s, but marriage and a child had intervened in each of their lives since they were classmates there.[2] Rebecca is now a student at Yale University, a filmmaker, and a fine writer in her own right, according to her mother.

By 1978 Walker had also published a second volume of poetry, *Revolutionary Petunias* (1973); a collection of short stories, *In Love and Trouble* (1973); and a second novel, *Meridian* (1976),[3] praised as one of the best about the freedom movement in the South. As a Guggenheim grant awarded her in 1978 started to run out, she and Allen sought a place that would allow her to write a third novel that had been on her mind for some time. They found it in Mendicino County, California, where the mountains reminded her of her native Georgia. The characters of *The Color Purple*,[4] rural folk who would not speak to her freely in New York or in San Francisco, were happy to come to her there. The proceeds from the sale of a second collection of stories, *You Can't Keep a Good Woman Down* (plus a retainer from *Ms.* for serving as a long-distance editor), freed her to cancel all lecture tours and public appearances for a year and to stay home, piece together a quilt, and listen to her characters tell their story. When it was written, she missed them so much that she brought several of them back in her 1989 novel *The Temple of My Familiar.*[5]

Walker speaks of her early writing as a means of survival, an alternative to despair. Over time, though, her writing has become not only a means of averting crisis but a means of achieving health. She told David Bradley in 1984, "I think writing really helps you heal yourself.

I think if you write long enough, you will be a healthy person. That is, if you write what you need to write, as opposed to what will make money, or what will make fame" (Bradley, 36). In writing *The Color Purple* she was fortunate enough to do all three.

In "Beauty: When the Other Dancer Is the Self," Walker recalls that her personal healing began when she was 27 and Rebecca was almost three. Her favorite brother, Bill, had paid to have the white scar tissue removed from her eye when she was 14. Yet a "bluish crater" still marked where it had been. She dreaded the day that Rebecca would notice it. Rebecca, however, grew up watching the children's television show "Big Blue Marble," with its opening shot of the earth as viewed from the moon. When her child's eyes finally focused on the spot, she pointed out very seriously, "Mommy, there's a *world* in your eye. . . . Mommy, where did you get that world in your eye?" Her mother's response:

For the most part the pain left then. . . . Crying and laughing I ran to the bathroom, while Rebecca mumbled and sang herself off to sleep. Yes indeed, I realized, looking into the mirror. There *was* a world in my eye. And I saw that it was possible to love it: that in fact, for all it had taught me of shame and anger and inner vision, I *did* love it. Even to see it drifting out of orbit in boredom, or rolling up out of fatigue, not to mention floating back at attention in excitement (bearing witness, a friend has called it), deeply suitable to my personality, and even characteristic of me.

That night I dream I am dancing. . . . As I dance, whirling and joyous, happier than I've ever been in my life, another bright-faced dancer joins me. We dance and kiss each other and hold each other through the night. The other dancer has obviously come through all right, as I have done. She is beautiful, whole and free. And she is also me. (*Gardens,* 393)

The little girl who had felt ugly and disfigured and alone had finally come through healthy and whole. Not all of her fictional characters do, but their struggle for wholeness is the stuff Walker's fictional world is made of.

Chapter Three
Boundaries of Self:
In Love and Trouble

In her 1988 collection of essays, *Living by the Word,* Walker states, "There is no story more moving to me personally than one in which one woman saves the life of another, and saves herself, and slays whatever dragon has appeared. And I know that, on a subconscious level, if not a conscious one, this is the work black women wish they were able to do all the time" (*Living,* 19). The 13 women who come to life on the pages of her first collection of short stories, *In Love and Trouble* (1973), unfortunately are not yet able to save themselves, let alone save others or triumph over dragons. One of the dragons that threatens these women is racism in its various individual and institutional forms. Another is their love of black men who use and abuse them. In the stories being in love often means being in trouble. Walker wrote in 1974, "In my new book *In Love and Trouble: Stories of Black Women,* 13 women—mad, raging, loving, resentful, hateful, strong, ugly, weak, pitiful, and magnificent, try to live with the loyalty to black men that characterizes all of their lives" (*Gardens,* 251).

At about the same time, while speaking at the 1973 Radcliffe symposium "The Black Woman: Myths and Realities," Walker was horrified to realize the extent to which black women still placed loyalty to black men above all else, including loyalty to themselves, a situation she termed "a dangerous state of affairs that has its logical end in self-destructive behavior" (*Gardens,* 318). She realized that while black women applauded the invincibility of the strong women of color she honored in "In Search of Our Mothers' Gardens," they seemed to have little sympathy for women whose personal struggles ended in defeat. Having struggled for health and wholeness herself, Walker saw the struggle as worthy of its place in fiction, although not all her female characters proved to be the dragonslayers they might have longed to be. Her first short story (unpublished), "The Suicide of an American Girl," is about a young black woman who turns on the gas and waits to die after she is raped by an African student angered by her independence. In some instances the women of *In Love and Trouble* lose a life-or-death struggle for survival; more often, however, it is psychological wholeness that eludes them.

Misplaced Loyalty, Misplaced Love

The search for psychological wholeness is at the heart of "Roselily," the opening story of *In Love and Trouble*. The story's title character has found a means of escape from her life of labor and single parenthood in Panther Burn, Mississippi, by marrying a black Muslim from Chicago. As they stand before a preacher on the front porch of her father's house, however, the words of their marriage ceremony interweave with Roselily's thoughts as she realizes the price she is about to pay for financial security and a future for her children.

Immediately following the "Dearly beloved" as the ceremony begins, "she dreams." In her dream, Roselily sees herself as a little girl in her mother's white robe and veil. The marriage is her chance to "be on top," for her children to be "at last from underneath the detrimental wheel" (*Trouble*, 4). Yet the life she foresees in Chicago promises to be a nightmare; the marriage veil will merge with the veil (*purdah*) she will have to wear as the wife of a Muslim. When she hears the phrase "to join this man and this woman," Roselily "thinks of ropes, chains, handcuffs, his religion. His place of worship. Where she will be required to sit apart with covered head" (*Trouble*, 4).

Isolated as they are from the rest of the ceremony by Roselily's intervening thoughts, the words "these two should not be joined" take on ominous significance. At the mention of union, she thinks not of her groom, but of her dead mother, to whom she still feels confusingly joined. The past, not the future, beckons her: "An arm seems to reach out from behind her and snatch her backward. She thinks of cemeteries and the long sleep of grandparents mingling in the dirt. She believes that she believes in ghosts" (*Trouble*, 6). Her husband will place her on a pedestal, but to her a pedestal is a stalk that has no roots. How does one make new roots? What happens to memories in a new life? As Zora Neale Hurston's protagonist Janie discovers in *Their Eyes Were Watching God*, life on a pedestal is lonely. Janie chooses to come down from her pedestal to love a man with whom she can exist on equal footing. Roselily is not to have that alternative. She realizes that she has been too eager to be done with the past, too impatient in seeking a new life in Chicago: "Impatient to see the South Side, where they would live and build and be respectable and respected and free. Her husband would free her. A romantic hush. Proposal. Promises. A new life! Respectable, reclaimed, renewed. Free! In robe and veil" (*Trouble,* 7).

Thus into her dream of freedom once more intrudes the veil, and then more words from the marriage ceremony, weighty with significance in their isolation and in their hint of bondage: "or forever hold." The marriage veil has been transformed into the *purdah,* the outward sign that in her womanhood she is inferior and that marriage is a binding, not a freeing. (The term *purdah* is significantly applied both to the veil and to the Muslim segregation of women it symbolizes.) She will have rest from her labor in a sewing factory—"her place will be in the home, he has said, repeatedly" (*Trouble,* 7)—yet when she is rested, there will be more babies, a thought that does not console her. She loves her new husband's pride, but is clearly in the act of sacrificing her own for the good of her children and for the peace that she should want: "She thinks she loves the effort he will make to redo her into what he truly wants. His love of her makes her completely conscious of how unloved she was before. This is something . . ." (*Trouble,* 7–8). Security may exist for her in Chicago, but not personal fulfillment. She will be remade into her husband's image of black womanhood.

Seldom in *In Love and Trouble* do we see Walker's women fighting back successfully against preconceived, stultifying, and restrictive notions of women's roles. When we are first introduced to Myrna of "Really, *Doesn't* Crime Pay?" through her journal entries, she has recently been released from the mental institution where she was sent for trying to decapitate her husband with a chain saw. (The noise woke him just in time.) In her aggressiveness, she might appear to be one of the dragonslayers, one of the fighters that Walker feels all women wish they could be, except her attempt at murder fails, as do all of her attempts at self-fulfillment.

Fulfillment comes for Myrna through her writing, yet her middle-class husband scorns her creative efforts: "No wife of mine is going to embarrass me with a lot of foolish, vulgar stuff" (*Trouble,* 15). He wants, rather, a mindless beauty accompanied by the sweet smells for which he is a glutton. If she wants something to occupy her time, she should go shopping or have a baby, both appropriately feminine activities and thus roughly equivalent in his mind. When she does follow his instructions and goes shopping, she stocks up on needless supplies of beauty aids: cold cream, lip gloss, wigs, and perfumes. Being the serious writer that she is, though, all the time she is haunting the mall she is grieving not for the children she will never have (she religiously uses birth control pills) but for her latest story, "dead in embryo" (*Trouble,* 16). She envisions a "serious" writer as one dressed in dungarees (again like Janie in *Their Eyes Were Watching God*), with messy hands and the smell of sweat.

When Mordecai Rich, "a vagrant, scribbling down impressions of the South," comes along and recognizes that her pretty brown hands are capable of writing "ugly, deep stuff," she is so grateful that she gives herself to him on the spot. She succumbs to his flattery because he sees beyond the sweet-smelling surface and asks to read everything that she has ever written—and she gives it all to him as readily as she gives him her body.

Myrna proves to be one of Walker's women whose loyalties are misdirected and destructive; she errs in her choice of both husband and lover. Before Mordecai's arrival, she feels trapped in her marriage, her "hands stilled by cowardice, [her] heart the heart of a slave" (*Trouble,* 16). Later, in the hospital, her husband's name, Ruel, reminds her of "Rule Britannia," with its celebration of dominion. In between, Mordecai betrays the trust she places in him not only by deserting her but also by stealing one of her stories, publishing it in a magazine under his own name. Mordecai is long gone, beyond her reach, so she turns her fury—and the chain saw—on her husband.

We see her at the end of the story (which is also its beginning) released from the hospital and sitting in the new red brick home where Ruel believes they can forget the past. She looks down at her "Helena Rubenstein hands" and explains to herself in her journal, "Since I am not a serious writer my nails need not be bitten off, my cuticles need not have jagged edges. I can indulge myself—my hands—in Herbessence nailsoak, polish, lotions, and creams. The result is a truly beautiful pair of hands: sweet-smelling, small, and soft . . ." (*Trouble,* 10–11). She has become the fragrant piece of fluff that her husband has always wanted, yet she has sweetened her body "to such an extent that even he (especially he) may no longer touch it. . . . I wait, beautiful and perfect in every limb, cooking supper as if my life depended on it. Lying unresisting on his bed like a drowned body washed to shore. But he is not happy. For he knows now that I intend to do nothing but say yes until he is completely exhausted" (*Trouble,* 12, 22–23).

Barbara Christian explains how even the small victory Myrna gains over her husband is earned at the loss of self: "In saying *yes* to mean *no,* Myrna uses the manipulative power of the word and secures some small victory. But it is a victory achieved from the position of weakness, for she has no alternative. Like countless southern belles, she has found that directness based on self-autonomy is ineffectual and that successful strategies must be covert. Such strategies demand patience, self-abnegation, falsehood. Thus at the end of this story, Myrna has yet to act."[1]

Myrna's and Roselily's husbands share the same limited perception of women's roles. Each expects no more of his wife than that she stay home and have babies. Neither wife is physically abused, yet both are denied psychological freedom and wholeness. Roselily is not sure what would constitute total fulfillment for her—"She wants to live for once. But doesn't know quite what that means" (*Trouble,* 8)—yet she senses with foreboding that whatever it is, there will be no room for it in her husband's home or in his religion. He will mold her, in any case, into the wife he wants. Myrna knows that fulfillment comes to her through her art, yet her husband thinks the role of artist is not a "correct" one. He succeeds in remaking her according to his image of what the wife of a successful businessman should be, but, ironically, the end product brings him no satisfaction.

The tragic Mrs. Jerome Franklin Washington III in "Her Sweet Jerome" (the fact that she is identified by no other name than her husband's is telling) falls so far short of what her husband thinks the modern black woman should be that he does not even consider her worth the effort it would take to remake her. From the squat roll of fat that constitutes her neck and the plump molelike freckles on her cheeks to her fat hairy legs and orange shoes, she is every inch an unlovable woman. When "little and cute" Jerome, a "studiously quiet schoolteacher" 10 years her junior, agrees to marry this homely hairdresser, his motives are suspect, especially when he beats her black and blue even before the wedding. However, she comes from that group known as "colored folks with money" and is able to buy his name if not his love with cars and clothes—and with money to support his real love: the revolution. So repulsed is Jerome by his wife's physical presence that she can occasionally get him to stay home quietly reading his paperbacks only if she promises not to touch him or talk to him.

When the malicious gossips at the beauty parlor smugly convince her that she has a rival, her jealousy drives her into the streets armed with axes, pistols, and knives in search of "the other woman." Her neighbors never know whom she will grab next, demanding, "You been messin' with my Jerome?" They only hope that when the final crack-up comes, it will be in the privacy of her home and not on their streets. She abandons all of her earlier attempts to make herself look pretty, if only in her own eyes: "Her firm bulk became flabby. Her eyes were bloodshot and wild, her hair full of lint, nappy at the roots and greasy on the ends. She smelled bad from mouth and underarms and elsewhere" (*Trouble*, 29). And Walker paints her as being as shallow intellectually as she is repulsive physically. The life that Jerome lives when he is with his "comrades" with their "African" names and their white friends is beyond her comprehension. She has no idea what goes on during the "workshops" they hold for "young toughs," but "she had long since stopped believing they had anything to do with cabinet-making or any other kind of woodwork" (*Trouble*, 31). When she bursts in on one of their meetings, expecting to find Jerome with his lover and finds herself instead in the middle of a political meeting, one of the "suspects" laughingly asks if she has come to join the revolution. She tries so hard to understand that she feels she is going to faint.

These "sisters" are not sexual rivals for Jerome's wife. In Jerome's mind, rather, they represent a level of existence to which she can never even aspire. Where they wear the "short kinky hair and large hoop earrings" of a new era, she spends her days in her beauty parlor processing hair to make it look like the white ideal of feminine beauty and prides herself on her pastel taffetas, umbrella hats, and elbow-length red satin gloves. Where they reject traditional religion, Jerome laughs at her each Sunday morning as she minces off to church on her high heels. Where they talk about the "slave trade," "violent over-throw," and "off[ing] de pig," she brags about how she doesn't "miss her 'eddicashion' as much as some did who had no learning and no money both together" (*Trouble*, 26). Because she is ugly, because she is ignorant, because she is not like them, Jerome feels justified in beating her and taking her money.

The truth about her "rival" finally dawns on her in a rush of panic as she searches the house for clues to the identity of Jerome's lover. She finds no scribbled names or phone numbers, no lipstick on his collars, but she does find under their bed a stack of dusty paperbacks that have fallen there over the months of their marriage—paperbacks about blackness and about revolution. When the truth strikes home, it is with "the belated rush of doomed comprehension. In a rush it came to her: 'It ain't no woman.' Just like that. It had never occurred to her there could be anything more serious." She realizes that she doesn't even know what the word *revolution* means, "unless it meant to go round and round, the way her head was going" (*Trouble*, 33–34).

She sets out to "kill" her paperback rivals, stacking them on Jerome's pillow and slashing them with her knives, then dousing them with kerosene and setting the marriage bed on fire. As the room burns, she backs into a corner "not near the open door" and screams as the fire starts to consume her flesh.

Misplaced loyalty. Misplaced love. Walker's women suffer the consequences—physical and psychological. And in both "Her Sweet Jerome" and "The Child Who Favored Daughter," which follows it in the volume, Walker introduces a theme she develops further in her first novel: how larger social issues intrude into the individual lives of black men and women to become the excuse for cruelty. At home Jerome's wife serves as a convenient punching bag while in public he ostensibly fights for the rights of blacks. Mrs. Washington is one of those women who get lost, or in this case trampled on, in the course of men's larger struggles. Of course, there is never any evidence that Jerome does anything more than read and talk about revolution, except that he spends his wife's inheritance on "something very big . . . like a tank" (*Trouble*, 31). Jerome is hardly the noble revolutionary. In his intellectual fight against oppression in general, he feels no remorse for his cruel and literal oppression of his wife.

Sisters/Spouses/Illusions of Soul

Who has the right to define what black women should be? Who sets the boundaries of self for these women? These questions recur throughout Walker's fiction. In "Roselily," "Really, *Doesn't* Crime Pay?," and "Her Sweet Jerome" that power seems to reside in black men. Yet these restrictions placed on black womanhood are not primarily personal or idiosyncratic, but rather common responses to the dictates of a racist and sexist culture. Roselily's husband is not so much defining his preference in a wife as reshaping this young Southern woman into an accepted image of the Muslim wife. Ruel's primary concern is that Myrna not embarrass him with her writing, that she fit the mold of the middle-class existence his financial success has made possible for her. Both men are more concerned about how the behavior of their wives will reflect on them than about the women as individuals. They do not want to be made to look bad by their women.

Definition of self becomes a function of where and with whom these women's loyalties lie. Is their primary loyalty to themselves or to others? At what point does a black woman say *no* to a definition of self being forced upon her from without? At what point does a black man? These answers, too, are bound up in societal expectations.

In "The Contrary Women of Alice Walker," Christian asks, "What happens when a black woman goes against convention, transgresses a deeply felt taboo, and says *no* directly and aloud?" (Christian, 38). In choosing a white lover, the Child in "The Child Who Favored Daughter," who is certainly no child, is saying no, thereby breaking a societal taboo, yet her choice is also a reflection on her father's manhood.

In looking for an excuse for hatred and abuse, the father in "The Child Who Favored Daughter" has to look no further than the color line.[2] When he discovers his daughter's affair, the revelation deals him a double blow: His daughter has committed the unforgivable sin of giving herself to the "master," and in doing so she has repeated the sin of her aunt, her father's sister, called only Daughter. As the father waits on the front porch with his shotgun within easy reach and his daughter's letter to her lover in hand, she slowly makes her way down the dusty lane from school bus to house, knowing that he knows. Her father flashes back to recall the sister she so resembles, the sister whom he so dearly loved but who also gave her love to a white man.

Daughter returned from her months with her lover, a white landowner, destroyed physically and mentally, and her fall almost destroyed her brother as well:

He was struck down, too, and cried many nights on his bed; for she had chosen to give her love to the very man in whose cruel, hot, and lonely fields he, her brother, worked. Not treated as a man, scarcely as well as a poor man treats his beast. . . . That she had given herself to the lord of his own bondage was what galled him! And that she was cut down so! He could not forgive her the love she gave that knew nothing of master and slave. For though her own wound was a bitter one and in the end fatal, he bore a hurt throughout his life that slowly poisoned him. (*Trouble,* 39–40)

The poison contaminates all of his future relationships with women: "The women in his life faced a sullen barrier of distrust and hateful mockery. He could not seem to help hating even the ones who loved him, and laughed loudest at the ones who cared for him, as if they were fools" (*Trouble,* 40). He exists in a world "where innocence and guilt [become] further complicated by questions of color and race," and he responds to that world by beating and crippling his wife because he chooses to believe, in spite of all evidence to the contrary, that she returns the white landlord's advances. The wife escapes by killing herself, but leaves behind the little girl who is a replica of Daughter.

The Child's love, like her aunt's, knows no barriers. Like the flowers that grow in any soil and "pledge no allegiance to banners of any man" (*Trouble*, 45), she loves where she will. Beaten by her father and left on the dirt floor of a shed overnight, she still will not deny the letter the next morning. She will leave rather than deny her love, yet the thought of her leaving is as unbearable to her father as the thought of her loving another man. For this story is dissected as well by the lines of impropriety that her father crosses.

Hints of incestuous longing on the father's part are evident as he recalls his love of his sister, his "first love"—recalls how in her madness she would sing and scream and tell them she was on fire, yet how she even then began "playing up to him in her cunning way, exploiting again his love. And he, tears never showing on his face, would let her bat her lashless eyes at him and stroke his cheeks with her frail, claw-like hand" (*Trouble*, 39). As father and daughter confront one another that morning, in his mind the line between daughter and sister blurs, just as in Walker's poetic interlude the line between sisters and wives does: "Unknowable women— / sisters / spouses / illusions of soul" (*Trouble*, 38). For a moment daughter and sister are one, and the father's feeling for his daughter at that moment is the feeling he had for his sister. What the daughter sees in his eyes is more terrifying than the darkness in the shed where she waited alone overnight. What she sees is his desire for her. This desire, not his indignation at her "love that knew nothing of master and slave," is what leads him to destroy her. When her rain-soaked blouse falls from her shoulders, leaving her young breasts bare, he gathers their fullness in his hands and "is suddenly burning with unnamable desire" (*Trouble*, 45). Drawing out his knife, he cuts off her breasts and flings them to the waiting dogs.

The foreshadowing of the Child's destruction is clear. Early in the story, as the father waits for his daughter to make the slow trip from school bus to house, she lingers along the way to say good-bye to the black-eyed Susans and buttercups that both she and her aunt have loved and that, in another poetic interlude, Walker calls "small, bright last wishes" (*Trouble*, 36). Above the father's head wasps buzz, building a nest. He knows that he must stop the young wasps from flying, just as he must stop his daughter before she flies: "Late in the summer, just as the babies are getting big enough to fly he will have to light paper torches and burn the paper houses down, singeing the wings of the young wasps before they get a chance to fly or to sting him as he sits in the cool of the evening reading his Bible" (*Trouble*, 37). The wasps are still there building their nest, however, after he has turned on himself the gun with which he threatened his daughter.

Institutional Boundaries

In other stories in *In Love and Trouble*, institutions, not individual black men, fail the women who put their trust in them, restricting their already circumscribed lives and limiting their ability to define the boundaries of their existence.

Rannie Mae Toomer in "Strong Horse Tea" puts her trust in the white medical world with its new miracle drugs to cure her little boy Snooks of his double pneumonia and whooping cough. She scoffs at the old home remedies, insistent that her child will have the benefits of modern medicine. Modern medicine does not find its way easily into a shack in the middle of a cow pasture, however, and the one messenger who links Rannie Mae to a world of hope beyond the pasture's encircling fence fails her. She stops the white mailman in a pouring rain, her dripping head and desperate plea for help an unwelcome intrusion into his rounds. Her message gets no further than Aunt Sarah, the old rootworker down the road, who is all the mailman thinks blacks need in the way of medical care. By stopping and yelling to Aunt Sarah to go help Rannie Mae the mailman does all that his conscience requires of him. He is in too much of a hurry to do anything more, eager to disassociate himself from the wet-goat smell of Rannie Mae and the disgusting touch of her hands on his shoulder.

As her son lies dying, Rannie Mae loses valuable time waiting for a doctor who will never come. Aunt Sarah wonders in despair, "When would this one know that she could only depend on those who would come" (*Trouble*, 93). Only when Aunt Sarah finally makes Rannie Mae understand that she is the only help coming does Rannie Mae in desperation thrust Snooks into her arms. According to Aunt Sarah, the only bit of home "magic" that might save the baby is a dose of "strong horse tea," horse urine. While Rannie Mae runs about the pasture trying to gather some in her shoe, Snooks draws his last breath.

In "Strong Horse Tea," Rannie Mae and her child are denied access to the white medical world. Her one link to that world, the mailman, lacks the compassion that might have meant the difference between life and death for Rannie Mae's son. In "The Welcome Table," the world of white religion is closed to an old, unnamed black woman who eventually finds her salvation outside the white church whose doors are closed to her.

No one knows why on this day, this late in her life, the old woman walked the half mile from her home to climb the steps of the white church she had never entered to take her seat there on the back pew. No one knows exactly what the minister said to her in the vestibule before she brushed past him. No one knows exactly what the usher said when he tried to get her to leave. Little is known about that day at all because, once it was over, no one ever talked about it. The white people on the steps and in the church that day could not know her reason for violating a social code she had lived with all her life. Walker tells us only that she was was "singing in her head" (*Trouble,* 84) and therefore was not looking when they came to take her away. Since the white churchgoers could not hear the singing and could read nothing in her face, "they gazed nakedly upon their own fear transferred; a fear of the black and the old, a terror of the unknown as well as of the deeply known" (*Trouble,* 81). What each witness feared influenced what he or she saw in the face of a solitary old black woman that day. "Some . . . saw cooks, chauffeurs, maids, mistresses, children denied or smothered in the deferential way she held her cheek to the side, toward the ground. Many of them saw jungle orgies in an evil place, while others were reminded of riotous anarchists looting and raping in the streets. Those who knew the hesitant creeping up on them of the law, saw the beginning of the end of the sanctuary of Christian worship, saw the desecration of Holy Church, and saw an invasion of privacy, which they struggled to believe they still kept" (*Trouble,* 82). For the whites in "The Welcome Table," faith has nothing to do with their treatment of this woman. Fear has everything to do with it.

The white church as an institution established and maintained by men (or, more significantly, by women in this case) fails the old black woman; her faith does not. Thrown out of the church, she looks out from the top of the steps and sees Jesus walking down the road looking just like the picture she stole from the Bible of a white woman for whom she worked. On his command of "Follow me," she falls in step beside him and walks down the highway, talking to Jesus, singing, and quietly looking up at the sky until death overtakes her. Perhaps the whites are right to fear the power of this seemingly harmless elderly

black woman who "perhaps . . . had known suffering" (*Trouble*, 81).
As she walks herself to death at the side of a Lord who to her is very
real, she tells Him how the doors of His church have been shut against
her. Walker dedicates the story to gospel singer Clara Ward and opens
it with the warning words of this spiritual:

> I'm going to sit at the Welcome table
> Shout my troubles over
> Walk and talk with Jesus
> Tell God how you treat me
> One of these days! (*Trouble*, 81)

Because of her faith, the old woman's death is actually one of relatively few moments of triumph in the collection. One of the others
comes in "The Revenge of Hannah Kemhuff" with the destruction of
Mrs. Holley, the white woman who once denied Mrs. Kemhuff the free
food that would have saved her children from starvation. That the government's food stamp program failed to save the Kemhuffs in spite of
the faith they had in it is another example of institutional failure. Mrs.
Kemhuff also feels God has failed her because He has allowed Mrs.
Holley to prosper. She tells Tante Rosie, the rootworker to whom she,
like Rannie Mae, finally turns in desperation, "God cannot be let to
make her happy all these years and me miserable. What kind of justice
would that be? It would be monstrous!" (*Trouble*, 67). In "The Welcome Table," the church fails the old woman, but she never loses the
faith in God that allows her to march off to glory at the side of a savior
no one else can see. Mrs. Kemhuff has given God His chance, and as
she nears death, she goes outside Christianity to seek revenge through
the powers of voodoo that Rannie Mae also turned to as a last resort.
She and the old woman in "The Welcome Table" find victory only in
death.

Another story in *In Love and Trouble* features a character in search of
a faith that will not force her to deny her own perceptions of self and
self-fulfillment. "Diary of an African Nun" is not a story of triumph,
however, but of eventual surrender to hopelessness and betrayal. The
young nun's struggle is an inner one, one put into words only in the
pages of her diary.

The young Ugandan was born in a village "civilized" by American
missionaries and was converted from her tribal religion to Catholicism.
Her use of quotation marks around the word *civilized* reveals her doubts

about what constitutes civilization. As a schoolgirl in her bright blue uniform, though, she longed to be like the priests and nuns. What she did not know was that they were not allowed to have children.

At age 20 she earned the right to wear the white habit, symbolizing her marriage to Christ. The habit worn by this beautiful young black woman is itself symbolized by the cloak of snow that covers her beloved Ruwenzori mountains, hiding—except for one brief period in the spring—the fecundity of the blackness underneath.

At night, alone in her room, the nun is torn between the chants of her Catholic faith and the even older tribal chants that reach her with the beat of the African drums. In her mind, she witnesses a fertility ritual around the village fire and struggles to determine which chant first spoke to her.

Must I still ask myself whether it was my husband, who came down bodiless from the sky, son of a proud father and flesh upon the earth, who first took me and claimed the innocence of my body? Or was it the drumbeats, messengers of the sacred dance of life and deathlessness on earth? Must I still long to be within the black circle around the red, glowing fire, to feel the breath of love hot against my cheeks, the smell of love strong about my waiting thighs! Must I still tremble at the thought of the passions stifled beneath this voluminous rustling snow! (*Trouble,* 115)

She imagines the words she would speak to Christ, her husband, to try to make him understand that there is more promise in the natural fruitfulness of the earth and its men and women than in the artificial spring of resurrection:

Dearly Beloved, let me tell you about the mountains and the spring. The mountains that we see around us are black, it is the snow that gives them their icy whiteness. In the spring, the hot black soil melts the crust of snow on the mountains, and the water as it runs down the sheets of fiery rock burns and cleanses the naked bodies that come to wash in it. It is when the snows melt that the people here plant their crops; the soil of the mountains is rich, and its produce plentiful and good.

What have I or my mountains to do with a childless marriage, or with eyes that can see only the snow. . . . (*Trouble,* 117)

What she says to him instead, however, is that she will serve him and say nothing "of [her] melancholia at [his] lack of faith in the spring" (*Trouble*, 117). As one of those who "civilize" the savage, she will help to kill the passion and perpetuate the barrenness:

My mouth must be silent, then, though my heart jumps to the booming of the drums, as to the last strong pulse of life in a dying world.

For the drums will soon, one day, be silent. I will help muffle them forever. To assure life for my people in this world I must be among the lying ones and teach them how to die. I will turn their dances into prayers to an empty sky, and their lovers into dead men, and their babies into unsung chants that choke their throats each spring.

In this way will the wife of a loveless, barren, hopeless Western marriage broadcast the joys of an enlightened religion to an imitative people. (*Trouble*, 118)

In "From an Interview," Walker speculated about how the world would have been different for black women had they read and taken to heart, since its publication in 1937, Zora Neale Hurston's *Their Eyes Were Watching God*. She asks in the 1974 essay, "Would they still be as dependent on material things—fine cars, furs, big houses, pots and jars of face creams—as they are today? Or would they, learning from Janie that materialism is the dragrope of the soul, have become a nation of women immune (to the extent that is possible in a blatantly consumerist society like ours) to the accumulation of things, and aware, to their core, that love, fulfillment as women, peace of mind, should logically come before, not after, selling one's soul for a golden stool on which to sit" (*Gardens*, 264). The women of *In Love and Trouble*, with the possible exception of Myrna, do not have even the middle-class equivalent of a golden stool to sit upon. They are still seeking those things that should most logically come first—love, fulfillment as women, and peace of mind. Few of them are totally successful in their search. Only in her later works does Walker create women richer in life's intangibles and more fulfilled according to their own definitions of selfhood.

Chapter Four

The Burden of Responsibility, the Flaw of Unforgiveness: *The Third Life of Grange Copeland*

In *In Love and Trouble* Walker explored the limitations placed on women's definitions of self and their often fruitless battles for physical security and psychological health. As Trudier Harris has so aptly pointed out, Walker's first novel, *The Third Life of Grange Copeland,* illustrates that there is danger to the black male as well in adopting someone else's definition of self.[1] Grange Copeland has been poisoned by the dehumanizing effects of the Southern sharecropping system in much the same way as the father in "The Child Who Favored Daughter." Yet a man who begins to accept that he is somehow less than human because another man or a whole society tells him so has no reason to resist the animal within him. A man who is denied power over his own life finds it easy to disavow the evil he does, even when the target of his abuse is the woman he loves. Still, Walker believes in the inviolability of the human soul, and that belief is at the heart of her first novel. In the afterword to the 1988 Pocket edition of *The Third Life of Grange Copeland* she writes, "I believe wholeheartedly in the necessity of keeping inviolate the one interior space that is given to all. I believe in the soul. Furthermore, I believe it is prompt accountability for one's choices, a willing acceptance of responsibility for one's thoughts, behavior and actions, that makes it powerful. The white man's oppression of me will never excuse my oppression of you, whether you are man, woman, child, animal or tree, because the self that I prize refuses to be owned by him. Or by anyone" ("Afterword," 345). This is the lesson that Grange Copeland has to learn.

Oppressed by white society, victims of the sharecropping system, Grange and his son Brownfield take out their frustrations by brutalizing their women, by becoming the brutes the white men who own their labor perceive them to be. Grange has to leave the South and travel to New York in the second of his three lives before he learns that he cannot blame the white man for his own failure to be a man, that to do so is to grant other men the power of gods. When he returns to the South in the third life that gives the novel its title and finds his son caught up in the same tragic cycle of brutality, he tries to teach him to take responsibility for his own mistakes, but no rebirth occurs to save the son.

Brutes and Brutality

The Third Life covers three generations of the Copeland family and a period of American history from the 1920s to the 1960s. W. Lawrence Hogue has summarized one view of that period that corresponds with Walker's selection, transformation, and arrangement of historical fact: "The American social structure turns the Black man into a beast—suppressing his human qualities and accenting his animal tendencies. The Black man, in turn, reflects his violent relation with his white landowner in his relations with his wife and son. He takes his anger and frustration out, not on the social system or the people who exercise its power but on his children and on the black woman, who, as he does in the master-servant relation, remains loyal and submissive."[2]

That Grange sheds his human characteristics in the presence of Shipley, the white man in whose fields he labors, comes through in Walker's images of masks and stone. At best Grange is a man of silence; when Shipley arrives in his truck at the end of the work day to collect the picked cotton, Brownfield sees his father don a mask "more impenetrable than his usual silence. . . . For when the truck came his father's face froze into an unnaturally bland mask, curious and unsettling to see. It was as if his father became a stone or a robot. A grim stillness settled over his eyes and he became an object, a cipher, something that moved in tense jerks if it moved at all" (*Copeland*, 8).

During the dulling cycle of the Copelands' weekly life together, Grange takes on animalistic traits. He spends the early part of each week recovering from the weekend's drunken binge. By Thursday, however, the gloom of his situation has overtaken him once more, and, animal-like, he stalks the house and swings from the rafters of the porch. By Friday he is in a stupor from the work and the sun. On Saturday Grange cleans up and escapes down the road into town and into the arms of his lover, the prostitute Josie, staggering home late Saturday night "threatening to kill his wife and Brownfield, stumbling and shooting off his shotgun," while his wife, Margaret, and his son, terrorized, hide in the woods. "Then Grange would roll out the door and into the yard, crying like a child in wrenching sobs and rubbing his whole head in the dirt. He would lie there until Sunday morning, when the chickens pecked around him, and the dog sniffed at him and neither his wife nor Brownfield went near him" (*Copeland*, 12).

Hogue writes, "On the one hand, *The Third Life* reproduces an established definition of manhood—taking care of self and family—that becomes the model for measuring the worth and value of the Afro-American male. On the other hand, the text places that definition of manhood in an Afro-American constellation where it has no chance to materialize" (Hogue, 56). Trapped in an unending cycle of debt, Grange gives the fatal shrug of resignation that shows he acknowledges his inability to care for his family. Brownfield sees it when he is 10 as his father looks appraisingly at the "sway-backed" cabin in which they live: "Grange stood with an arm across the small of his back, soldier fashion, and with the other hand made gestures toward this and that of the house, as if pointing out necessary repairs. There were very many. . . . While his son watched, Grange lifted his shoulders and let them fall. Brownfield knew this movement well; it was the fatal shrug. It meant that his father saw nothing about the house that he could change and would therefore give up gesturing about it and he would never again think of repairing it" (*Copeland*, 13–14). He gave the same shrug when he gave up hope of sending his son to school, when he gave up hope even of buying Margaret the new dress she needed. Five years later, when Brownfield is 15, his father shrugs off all responsibility and deserts his wife and child.

At one point in "The Child Who Favored Daughter," Walker says of the father, "He knows that as one whose ultimate death must conform to an aged code of madness, resignation is a kind of dying" (*Trouble*, 44). Resigned to his inability to control his life or that of his wife and son, Grange walks away. This "death" ends his first life.

According to Hogue's analysis of the historical milieu of the Copelands' story, Margaret is one of those black women who are submissive and loyal because they have such limited control over their own lives. Dependent on their husbands, such women lose respect for themselves and their husbands. As a child, Brownfield watches a transformation take place in his mother and blames Grange for it. In the beginning he loves his mother yet sees her "like a dog in some ways. She didn't have a thing to say that did not in some way show her submission to his father" (*Copeland*, 5). The one thing Margaret will not do is to prostitute herself, even to free her family from years of debt. Brownfield's city cousins tell him that Grange tried to convince her to "sell herself" for that purpose. Brownfield wonders, "Maybe his mother was as scared of Grange as he was, terrified by Grange's tense composure. Perhaps she was afraid he would sell her anyway, whether she wanted to be sold or not. That could be why she jumped to please him" (*Copeland*, 11).

During the many months before his final departure when Grange leaves her every Saturday to go off down the road to the juke joint and to Josie's bed, the one place where he can still feel like a man, at first Margaret cleans herself up and sits waiting for guests who never come; eventually she starts to follow Grange down the same road. Soon she starts arriving home the next morning in the same truck that carries the man who turns Grange to stone. Having refused to "sell herself," Margaret now chooses to give herself freely to the man who drives the truck or to anyone else. The "comforting odors of cooking and soap and milk" Brownfield once associated with his mother "when he had loved her" have been replaced in Margaret's new life by her "new painted good looks and new fragrance of beds, of store-bought perfume and of gin" (*Copeland*, 16). Her new life produces a new son, and as Brownfield recognizes, "From its odd coloration its father might have been every one of its mother's many lovers" (*Copeland*, 19). When Grange has been gone three weeks, Margaret knows he is really gone this time. Unable to envision a life without him, she poisons herself and her oddly colored baby.

As Klaus Ensslen observes in his essay "Collective Experience and Individual Responsibility," Margaret is one of the women Walker describes as suspended—"suspended in a time in history when the options for Black women were severely limited . . . [who] either kill themselves or . . . are used up by the man, or by the children, or by . . . whatever the pressures against them."[3] Ensslen writes:

Margaret drastically exemplifies this state of suspension without creative outlet, devoid of real options, when we see her driven into the radical moral resignation of suicide. On the other hand, Margaret's spontaneous reaction to her husband's desertion already contains the seed for an as yet unseized opportunity for self-definition equating or even transcending Grange's self-estimate at that point: while he goes through the accelerating motion of flight, she seems to be able to discover—even if only fleetingly—a positive form of self-directed joy in living, in sexual self-assertion—comparable to what Alice

Walker has described in other women when they take recourse to flower gardens or the knitting of quilts. Margaret thus embodies a kind of germinal unconscious attempt at feminine self-realization.[4]

If Margaret's attempt at self-realization is unconscious, it is also unsuccessful. She has not achieved a level of independence from Grange that will enable her to feel she can survive without him. In keeping with Walker's observations about other "suspended" women, the seed of self-actualization that Margaret keeps alive will come to fruition only later, in her granddaughter Ruth.

In the meantime, the 15-year-old Brownfield returns from Margaret's funeral wearing the same stony mask his father wore, turns his back on his father's house, and starts both literally and figuratively down the same road.

Cycles of Despair

Fate leads Brownfield not only down the same road but into the same juke joint earlier frequented by his father, quickly into Josie's bed, and soon into her daughter Lorene's bed. By one definition of manhood Brownfield has come of age—in demand by two women, each of whom uses him to inspire jealousy in the other.

He soon learns there is more to manhood, however, in the presence of Mem, Josie's educated niece and ward. Finding himself suddenly in love with this young schoolteacher, so like the mother he wishes his had been, he assumes an adult's responsibility for the first time and finds a job that will give him the financial independence to support a wife. Unfortunately, in committing himself to sharecropping for two years, he enters the same trap his father felt compelled to escape. A week later the newlywed Brownfield and Mem ride off on a wagon to start their new life together with Brownfield blindly promising, "We ain't always going to be stuck down here, honey," and Mem "looking and smiling at him with gay believing eyes, full of love" (*Copeland*, 49).

Thus, early in their relationship are planted seeds not of creativity but of destruction. Brownfield is never able truly to assume responsibility for himself and his family in a way that will free them from the cycle of despair into which he was born; his is to be a failed attempt at responsibility. Mem, on the other hand, believes too fully in a man unworthy of her trust.

Three years later Brownfield and Mem, now with two children, are still on the same farm and deep in debt, but Brownfield can still escape his frustrations in Mem's nurturing arms: "He did not care what anybody thought about it, but she was so good to him, so much what he needed, that her body became his shrine and he kissed it endlessly, shamelessly, lovingly, and celebrated its magic with flowers and dancing; and, as the babies, knowing their places beside her as well as life, sucked and nursed at her bosom, so did he, and grew big and grew firm with love, and grew strong." Love, of course, produces more babies and the burden of more responsibility, "another link in the chain that held him to the land and to a responsibility for her and her children" (*Copeland,* 50).

The year soon comes when Brownfield gives the "fatal shrug" his father gave. Brownfield gives his own fatal shrug of hopelessness the year he has to teach his five-year-old daughter, Daphne, how to mop the cotton plants with arsenic to kill the boll weevils: ". . . that year of awakening roused him not from sleep but from hope that someday she would be a fine lady and carry parasols and wear light silks. That was the year he first saw how his own life was becoming a repetition of his father's. He could not save his children from slavery; they did not even belong to him. . . . That was the year he accused Mem of being unfaithful to him, of being used by white men, his oppressors; a charge she tearfully and truthfully denied" (*Copeland,* 54).

They become transients, moving from one sharecropper's cabin to another until Brownfield is left feeling that he has no control over his own life and therefore must assume no responsibility: "For Brownfield, moving about at the whim of a white boss was just another example of the fact that his life, as it was destined, had 'gone haywire,' and he could do nothing about it. He jumped when the crackers said jump, and left his welfare up to them. He no longer had, as his father had maintained, even the desire to run away from them" (*Copeland,* 59).

The idea of the black man taking out his frustrations on the black woman because he dare not risk taking them out on a white person of either gender is not a new idea. Hurston popularized the image of the black woman of an earlier time as "the mule of the world." The image is based on the assumption that the black woman has been the only human creature more helpless than a black man living in a white world. Mem Copeland, however, breaks the mold of the black woman brutalized because of her helplessness. Mem, rather, is the target of Brownfield's abuse because her power, not her lack of it, allies her with

Brownfield's white oppressors. The source of her power is her educa-tion—an education Brownfield does not have:

> His crushed pride, his battered ego, made him drag Mem away from school-teaching. Her knowledge reflected badly on a husband who could scarcely read and write. It was his great ignorance that sent her into white homes as a domestic, his need to bring her down to his level! It was his rage at himself, and his life and his world that made him beat her for an imaginary attraction she aroused in other men, crackers, although she was no party to any of it. His rage and his anger and his frustration ruled. And she accepted all his burdens along with her own and dealt with them from her own greater heart and greater knowledge. He did not begrudge her the greater heart, but he could not forgive her the greater knowledge. It put her closer, in power, to *them*, than he could ever be. (*Copeland*, 55)

Walker calls Brownfield Mem's "Pygmalion in reverse." He sets out to break her, starting with her speech, demeaning her and humiliating her in front of his friends until she drops her educated dialect for the old one she shared with them. Her schoolbooks become the kindling to start the daily fire in whatever shack he has condemned his wife and their growing family to live. Only once does he go for a midwife when the time comes for one of his children to be born; the other times he is too drunk or it is too cold. Mem becomes haggard and ugly by his beatings: "Everything about her he changed, not to suit him, for she had suited him when they were married. He changed her to something he did not want, could not want, and that made it easier for him to treat her in the way he felt she deserved. A fellow with an ugly wife can ignore her, he reasoned. It helped when he had to beat her too" (*Copeland*, 57).

Grange's wife, Margaret, found her alternative to despair in suicide. Ironically perhaps, she killed herself because she loved Grange so much that she could not live without him and could not forgive herself the sin of infidelity. Mem goes on living with Brownfield in what Walker terms "a harmony of despair" (*Copeland*, 59) until she strikes back—once—for the sake of their three children.

Mem finally takes the initiative and signs a lease on a house in town. This reminder that Brownfield never learned to read and write well enough to sign a lease, together with knowing that Mem has assumed the responsibility of caring for the family, is a blow to his ego. She has gotten a job and announces she will take the children to live in town

whether he goes or not. His typical response is to laugh at her attempt
to better herself and once more to beat her into submission. When
talking fails to convince him that she is serious, he wakes up, hung
over, one morning to find a shotgun pointed at his testicles and Mem
finally mad enough to pull the trigger if pushed to it. She has sent the
children off to church, and Brownfield realizes that she has little to
lose. She tells him, "Ain't nobody here but us chickens. Ain't nobody
round to know or care whether one of us gets fried." Brownfield responds with a moan of "Oh, Lawd," and when Mem tells him, "Call
on the one you serves, boy! . . . Call on the one you serves," the image
that pops into Brownfield's head is that of the only "god" Brownfield
serves: Captain Davis, the white man who has just fired him (*Copeland*,
93).

Called to account by a wife who has had enough, Brownfield tearfully but characteristically tries to shift the burden of guilt for all the
wrong that he has done onto the white man: "'Mem, . . . you know
how hard it is to be a black man down here, . . . Mem, baby, the
white folks just don't let nobody *feel* like doing right. . . . What can
a man *do?*' . . . 'He can quit wailing like a old seedy jackass!' she said,
hitting him over the head with the gun. Brownfield skidded in the
mess on the floor and lay too weak to move" (*Copeland*, 95).

In her one triumphant moment, as her husband lies on the floor
groveling in his own blood and vomit, Mem delivers her own "Ten
Commandments," her rules of conduct for the new home she is going
to control. Among them are these: "Eight, you going to take the blame
for every wrong thing you do and stop blaming it on me and Captain
Davis and Daphne and Ornette and Ruth and everybody else for fifty
miles around. Ninth, you going to respect my house by never coming
in it drunk. And tenth, you ain't never going to call me ugly or black
or nigger or bitch again, 'cause you done seen just what this black ugly
nigger bitch can do when she gits mad!" All Brownfield can do is cower
against the door and sob, "Yes, ma'am" (*Copeland*, 95–97).

With life in town come such comforts as indoor plumbing and electric lights, conveniences the Copeland children had never known in the
1940s. With life in town comes a job for Mem, and one for Brownfield, too, that gets him out of the damp of the Davis dairy and lets
him regain his health. He lies in wait, however, for Mem to lose hers,
and again her "greater heart" leads her into the trap he sets. He forces
two pregnancies upon her, and although the babies do not live, her
pregnancies take away her health and her chance of employment, and

when the rent goes unpaid and they lose the house, Brownfield has won. His reasons for intentionally bringing his family down once again are those of a man who places his pride before his family's welfare and even his own: "If he had done any of it himself, if he had insisted on the move, he might not have resisted the comfort, the feeling of doing better-ness with all his heart. As it was, he could not seem to give up his bitterness against his wife, who had proved herself smarter, more resourceful than he, and he complained about everything often and loudly, secretly savoring thoughts of how his wife would 'come down' when he placed her once more in a shack" (*Copeland,* 103).

He moves Mem and their daughters back to the shack originally intended for them, with Mem too ill and weak to do more than threaten, "I'm going to git well again, and git work again, and when I do I'm going to leave you." Like Walker's own mother, Mem has prided herself on the flowers that have prospered under her nurturing no matter where her family was forced to live. This time, however, "dispiritedly she threw a few flower seeds in the moist rich soil around the woodpile. Never again did she intend to plant flowers in boxes or beds" (*Copeland,* 112).

True to her word, Mem does get well and hold a job as a domestic even when Brownfield loses his once more. The Jewish man she works for pays her well and is even kind enough on occasion to drive her home after dark. There is never any hint of anything sexual between Mem and her white boss (Mem has never been guilty of the infidelity Brownfield has accused her of), but the sight of her getting out of the white man's car one Christmas Eve reminds Brownfield of the image of his mother climbing out of a white man's truck many years before. For once in his life Brownfield feels totally in control of his own actions. Hating Mem for being strong enough once more to leave him and linking her in his anger with the mother who also deserted him, Brownfield waits only until she enters the circle of light from the front porch and fires his shotgun into her face.[5]

A Child of the Future

Walker could have ended the novel with Mem's death, but the title of the book suggests that this is, after all, Grange's story, not Brownfield's, and there remain the three children of this tragic marriage to inspire questions about the future. Grange's return makes the novel a study in contrast between the man who sees the error of his ways and the one who never does; between the one who eventually learns that a man's definition of self comes from within, not from some "cracker," and the one who never learns that lesson. The remainder of the book also develops the character of Grange's granddaughter Ruth, the precursor of later Walker women who have a chance to overcome brutality and injustice to survive "whole."

Grange reappears before the birth of this third granddaughter, a benevolent grandfather almost impossible to identify as the taciturn man behind the mask of stone of his first life who could not even bear to touch his son in parting. The second half of the book reiterates Walker's point about blame, already effectively illustrated by the events of the first half. Grange's story, however, and that of his granddaughter, are necessary to complete Walker's point about forgiveness.

As Brownfield sits in prison, the only justification he can find for murder is that he likes plump women and Mem's skinniness was more proof that he was unable to provide for her. If his fatal weakness, which he never recognizes, is that he can never fully accept the blame for his failure as a provider and as a human being, Mem's was that she was too willing to forgive and, in her forgiveness, all too human and therefore weak: "If she had been able to maintain her dominance over him perhaps she would not stand now so finished, a miniature statue, in his mind, but her inherent weakness, covered over momentarily by the wretched muscular hag, had made her ashamed of her own seeming strength. And without this strength, the strength to kill his ass, to make him wallow continually in his own puke, she was lost. Her weakness was forgiveness, a stupid belief that kindness can convert the enemy" (*Copeland,* 162). The one enemy that Grange can neither convert nor forgive is not ultimately, in spite of his avowed hatred for the entire white world, the white man, but his son, Brownfield.

With her mother dead and her father in prison for the murder, Ruth goes to live with Grange and Josie, whose money from the sale of her juke joint financed their farm. Grange willingly shoulders the burden of teaching Ruth the hatred that will enable her to survive, yet he can never bring himself to tell her the one story from his past—his second life—that would convince her that he hates whites as completely as he professes. He cannot tell her how he let a pregnant white woman drown in an icy pond in Central Park, how he tried to save her, but walked away once she rejected the hand that he held out to her because it was black, calling him "nigger" with her last breath.

Grange's first response to his "murder" of the white woman was to feel that "he had stumbled on the necessary act that black men must commit to regain, or to manufacture their manhood, their self-respect. They must kill their oppressors. . . . He was like a tamed lion who at last tasted blood. There was no longer any reason not to rebel against people who were not gods. His aggressiveness, which he had vented only on his wife, and his child, and his closest friends, now asserted itself in the real hostile world" (*Copeland,* 153–55).

Grange is never able fully to accept the United States as anything other than a hostile world, but he quickly realizes that fighting every white man he meets is not to be his way: "Each man would have to free himself, he thought, and the best way he could. For the time being, he would withdraw completely from them, find a sanctuary, make a life that need not acknowledge them, and be always prepared, with his life, to defend it, to protect it, to keep it from whites, inviolate" (*Copeland,* 155).

Grange believes that the reformation of America is impossible, and the only way blacks can feel "free and easy and at home" is to leave this country. Ruth, the representative of the future, however, believes in the feasibility of change:

"Maybe it would be better if something happened to change everything; made everything equal; made us feel *at home,*" said Ruth.

"They can't undo what they done and we can't forget it or forgive."

"Is it so hard to forgive 'em if they don't do bad things no more?"

"I honestly don't believe they *can* stop," said Grange, "not as a group anyhow." He lounged back in his chair and stuck a hand in his pocket. "Even if they could," he said slowly, "it'd be too late. I look in my heart for forgiveness and it just ain't there." (*Copeland,* 210)

The first step toward forgiveness is the proper assigning of blame. With only occasional stumbling, Grange is able to take that step. When Brownfield is released after seven years in prison, unchanged by his experiences in or out of prison, Grange tries one last time to force him to take that first step toward facing his own culpability:

By George, I *know* the danger of putting all the blame on somebody else for the mess you make out of your life. I fell into the trap myself! And I'm bound to believe that that's the way the white folks can corrupt you even when you done held up before. 'Cause when they got you thinking that they're to blame for *every*thing they have you thinking they's some kind of gods! You can't do nothing wrong without them being behind it. You gits just as weak as water,

no feeling of doing *nothing* yourself. Then you begins to think up evil and
begins to destroy everybody around you, and you blames it on the crackers.
Shit! Nobody's as powerful as we make them out to be. We got our own *souls,*
don't we? (*Copeland,* 207)

The willingness to forgive, like the willingness to accept blame,
ultimately must be measured in terms of the strength of the individual
soul. Even in old age Grange believes that the spoiling of the human
soul is what makes forgiveness impossible, that his began to spoil years
ago when he refused to forgive his young wife, Margaret, for seeking
solace in the arms of other men, and that the spoilage was complete
one December night when he walked away from a drowning woman,
condemning to death both her and her unborn child. Ruth, who has
been the sole recipient of the largesse of Grange's soul, argues playfully
that he actually caught his soul in the nick of time, just before it
spoiled completely. His inability to forgive, however, convinces him
that he failed to catch it in time.

Feeling that he himself is beyond redemption—with only a numb-
ness in his heart where the ability to forgive once resided, Grange
wants to preserve Ruth's soul in its youthful freshness. He longs to
shelter her always behind the barbed-wire barrier that he has erected
between her and the impersonal cruelty of the outside world. Nevertheless, that outside world crosses his barrier one day in the form of
four civil rights workers who leave Grange feeling that he has been
asleep for 40 years. If the type of social change that these young man
and women believe in so completely is truly possible, perhaps spiritual
change is possible too.

The two couples—one black, one white—have come to persuade
Grange to register to vote. What shocks Grange out of his years of
waking sleep is that the black husband and wife are not outside agitators but young people from his home county. They inform him that
blacks are voting in Green County and that they will soon even run for
office. Grange remains skeptical but envies their idealistic belief in the
possibility of change. He has not changed to the point where he can
offer the white couple the hospitality of his front porch, but he does
give the four a watermelon as a parting gift, and "when he wave[s]
good-bye he wave[s] to all of them" (*Copeland,* 242).

Ruth watches the Atlanta civil rights marches on television and decides that she agrees with the marchers that it just might be possible
to change the "crackers'" minds. Her grandfather is glad that such

hope exists unspoiled in the minds of the young, but what he really wants is for someone to change people like Brownfield.

For one brief moment as Brownfield prepares to fight Grange for custody of 16-year-old Ruth, he wishes that he could ask Mem's forgiveness; for once he acknowledges his own guilt. He is repulsed when he hears Josie echo his own constant blaming of the white man. The moment comes and goes quickly. He decides, as always, that there is nothing that he can do; one final time he gives his fatal shrug. He wants Ruth for the same reason that he would want any other possession: she is his. Besides, he wants to hurt Grange for deserting him. He never considers changing; he never considers taking Ruth into his home and simply being kind to her.

In the final chapter Grange shoots and kills Brownfield rather than let him have custody of Ruth. Grange, in turn, is shot for his crime. Ruth survives because, in leaving her unarmed to wait for his killers, Grange gives the killers no excuse for harming her. This is one time that, for her, a gun is not the way.

Unquestionably Ruth is going to live in a changed world—changed by the absence of her grandfather, who on the last day of his life still looks to his granddaughter like "Ruth's idea of God," but changed as well by people like the civil rights workers, who believe that working for the future is more important than assigning blame for past injustices. Ruth counts herself among the ones willing to forgive whites "if they don't do bad things no more."

The novel is thus as much about spiritual change as about social change, and it represents a move beyond *In Love and Trouble* in its portrayal of relations between black men and black women. Margaret died because she could never forgive herself; Mem, because she was too willing to forgive. Ruth, however, refuses to be the martyr Mem was. She chooses to live with the flaw of unforgiveness rather than to believe that Brownfield is capable of change. That toughness, that willingness to be unforgiving when necessary, combined with the compassion that makes forgiveness possible once it has been earned, is Ruth's defense against the future. The combination is what will enable her to survive whole rather than merely survive.

Walker's initial draft of *The Third Life of Grange Copeland* began with Ruth a civil rights lawyer in Georgia. Walker felt, however, that such a story would be "too recent, too superficial—everything seemed a product of the immediate present" (*Gardens,* 256). In bringing in the grandfather, she gave the novel the depth of generations. Ruth is a product of her past, but she is also a child of the future, even though Walker finally decided not to specify that future. She achieves a self-realization, a definition of self, that moves her beyond most of Walker's earlier women and that looks ahead to some of the spiritual and psychological triumphs of her later ones.

Chapter Five

Ashes among the Petunias: *Revolutionary Petunias* and *Meridian*

The main character in Walker's brief story "Petunias," which appears in her 1981 volume *You Can't Keep a Good Woman Down,* is killed in an explosion after her son comes home from Vietnam determined to teach her to make bombs. When she first begins agitating in support of the civil rights movement, she awakens one morning to find that whites have unearthed the grave of her mother, a slave, and scattered her ashes over the flower bed, a splintery leg bone falling among the petunias. Not all of Walker's "revolutionaries" are political activists, however. Rather, Walker calls *Revolutionary Petunias,* her 1973 collection of poems, winner of the Lillian Smith Award and nominee for the National Book Award, more generally "a celebration of people who will not cram themselves into any ideological or racial mold" (*Gardens,* 268). These are individualists who look to a future when all people, like the hardy petunias, can bloom, a thought that must not be forgotten even in the midst of the bloodiest revolution.

In "From an Interview," Walker explains how petunias came to be for her an image of survival.

Thirty-seven years ago, my mother and father were coming home from somewhere in their wagon—my mother was pregnant with one of my older brothers at the time—and they passed a deserted house where one lavender petunia was left, just blooming away in the yard (probably to keep itself company)—and my mother said Stop! let me go and get that petunia bush. And my father, grumbling, stopped, and she got it, and they went home, and she set it out in a big stump in the yard. It never wilted, just bloomed and bloomed. Every time the family moved (say twelve times) she took her petunia—and thirty-seven years later she brought me a piece of that same petunia bush. It had never died. Each winter it lay dormant and dead-looking, but each spring it came back, more lively than before. (*Gardens,* 268)

Walker claims that all of her characters in *Revolutionary Petunias* are shouting, "Stop! I want to get that petunia!" and that because of this they are made to suffer: "They are told that they do not belong, that they are not wanted, that their art is not needed, that nobody who is 'correct' could love what they love. Their answer is resistance, without much commentary; just a steady knowing that they stand at a point where—with one slip of the character—they might be lost, and the bloom they are after wither in the winter of self-contempt" (*Gardens,* 268–69).

One character who does not belong is Sammy Lou of Rue, the main character in the title poem of *Revolutionary Petunias,* who uses a hoe to murder her husband's murderer. She laughs in disbelief when unknown sonneteers label her a militant. According to Walker, Sammy Lou is the most "incorrect" of characters. She is not the typical heroine, but rather a farmer's wife who names her children after American Presidents, First Ladies, and John Wesley. Sammy Lou simply reaches the point where she will take no more, fights back, and wins, even though her reward is death in the electric chair. She is even "incorrect" enough not to realize the absurdity of trying to bring some color into her drab world by means of the flowers that she raises. On the way to the electric chair, she has one piece of advice, to respect the word of God, and one request, that her listeners water her flowers—petunias, of course.

Although Walker terms Sammy Lou a rebel rather than a revolutionary because hers is an isolated act of rebellion, Sammy Lou is linked in her "incorrectness" with Meridian Hill, the title character of Walker's 1976 novel of the turbulent 1960s, which seeks to define the revolution and the artist's role in time of revolution.[1]

Karen F. Stein has argued in "*Meridian*: Alice Walker's Critique of Revolution" that between the time Walker affirmed the value of the movement in "The Civil Rights Movement: What Good Was It?" and the time she wrote *Meridian,* she had had to revise her appraisal: "Thus, while she wrote of the Civil Rights Movement with unreserved approval in 1967, she would later contend that it continued to oppress women and so failed in its mission of human liberation. . . . Activists merely turned political rhetoric to their own ends while continuing to repress spontaneous individuality. To overcome this destructiveness, Walker reaches for a new definition of revolution. Her hope for a just society inheres not merely in political change, but in personal transformation."[2] According to Stein, Walker's new definition of true revolution, as it applies to Meridian Hill, is the struggle with the recalcitrant self. Before Meridian can successfully define her role within the revolution, she must first successfully define herself: "In order to live, Meridian rejects the temptations of conventional middle-class life, the conventional women's roles of dutiful daughter, wife, mother, lover. But she must reject as well the contemporary temptation of martyrdom and false revolutionary consciousness, for these roles are death masks" (Stein, 140).

Mothers and Daughters

Because *Meridian* is the story of one young woman's coming of age during the civil rights movement, the temptation to look for autobiographical elements is inevitable. Like Walker, Meridian has doors opened for her by means of a scholarship to a black women's college in Atlanta (not Spelman, but Saxon, with all the associations the term *Anglo-Saxon* implies). There she finds herself immersed in the activism of the 1960s—and has an abortion. Later Meridian suddenly appears to be at school briefly in the North, a move not explained in the novel, but one that parallels Walker's own transfer to Sarah Lawrence. The bulk of the novel, however, relates Meridian's movements about the South once she leaves school and joins the ranks of those trying to bring about social and political change through nonviolent means, the sorts of activities Walker herself became involved with during her summers in Georgia and Mississippi.

From that point on, however, fact and fiction diverge. Meridian is forced into an unfulfilling marriage by the birth of an unwanted child. Meridian's relationship with her mother is certainly not the nurturing relationship Walker has had with her own mother and that she has written about so movingly. How much of the heart and soul, how many of the thoughts and feelings of Meridian Hill are those of Alice Walker only Walker herself knows. Her own experiences inevitably enrich the characterization. Certainly some critical choices in Walker's life seem mirrored in her fictional creation. Like Walker herself and like Walker's foremothers in "In Search of Our Mothers' Gardens" who turned to art as an alternative to despair, Meridian eventually turns to art, but not before she considers death as an escape from her "winter of self-contempt," the burden of guilt that she bears.

Meridian's guilt is multifaceted. One of its major sources is established through a flashback early in the novel when we see 13-year-old Meridian in church on the day that she, as she terms it, "loses" her mother because she is unable to go forward and confess Christ as her savior, unable to do the "correct" thing. Her mother is linked with those strong black women who dragged their children to church in Walker's autobiographical poem "In These Dissenting Times" in *Revolutionary Petunias*.

Even at 13 death looms as a very real alternative for Meridian. The voice that she hears above all else is her father's from the choir loft, singing of death and his resignation to it. Drunk with the sound of her father's voice, she knows that she might have said anything, but the one thing that her mother most wants to hear is the one thing that she cannot say because "for all that her father sang beautifully, heart-breakingly, of God, she sensed he did not believe in Him in quite the same way her mother did" (*Meridian*, 29). She chooses her father's rationality over her mother's willing ignorance and in the process feels her mother's love withdrawn from her forever: "She struggled to retain her mother's hand, covering it with her own, and attempted to bring it to her lips. But her mother moved away, tears of anger and sadness coursing down her face. Her mother's love was gone, withdrawn, and there were conditions to be met before it would be returned. Conditions Meridian was never able to meet" (*Meridian*, 30).

Meridian spends years trying to expiate the guilt she feels for having failed her mother. Her family history is one of mothers who sacrificed even life itself for their children. Mrs. Hill's great-great-grandmother was a slave whose two children were sold. The third time she stole them back, her master agreed that she could keep them if she would take full responsibility for feeding them. The children survived into their teens on a diet of nuts, berries, and fish, until their mother died of slow starvation and they were sold after all. Mrs. Hill's own mother made a bargain with her hard-hearted husband that their daughter would be allowed to go to school only if the mother raised the annual $12 tuition. This she did by taking in laundry, and one of Mrs. Hill's first paychecks as a schoolteacher went to buy her mother's coffin.

Believing that it is death not to love one's mother, Meridian continues to see her mother as Black Motherhood personified, in spite of Mrs. Hill's failures as a mother. And, indeed, Mrs. Hill is a failure as a mother. She realizes too late that children are a trap, that a mother's personal life ends with the birth of her first child. Children are Mrs. Hill's—and later Meridian's—own form of slavery, a burden to be borne. Mrs. Hill sacrifices for her children, as did her mother and her great-great-grandmother before her, but "in the ironing of her children's clothes she expended all the energy she might have put into openly loving them" (*Meridian*, 79).

Many of the oppressed slave women Walker wrote about in "In Search of Our Mothers' Gardens" found outlets for their stifled creativity by adorning their homes through whatever modest domestic means were available. Even these outlets do not work for Meridian's mother: "She never learned to cook well, she never learned to braid hair prettily or to be in any other way creative in her home. She could have done so, if she had wanted to. Creativity was in her, but it was refused expression. It was all deliberate. A war against those to whom she could not express her anger or shout, 'It's not fair!' " (*Meridian*, 51). Her few artistic efforts are failures. Out of crepe paper and wire hangers, she fashions useless artificial flowers, and out of scraps of cloth, prayer pillows large enough for one knee only.

When, even as a child, Meridian tries to explain to her mother the vague guilt she feels for being a burden, the literal minded Mrs. Hill suspects a much more tangible source of her guilt. Her question is always the same: "Have you stolen anything?" Without having adequate words to explain her theft, Meridian knows that she has: "It was for stealing her mother's serenity, for shattering her mother's emerging self, that Meridian felt guilty from the very first, though she was unable to understand how this could possibly be her fault" (*Meridian*, 51). Meridian also knows that she would have stopped far short of the sacrifices made in the name of motherhood by those who have preceded her.

Meridian early becomes a mother herself, partly because her mother fails to teach her the most basic biological facts, thinking that her admonition to "be sweet" is enough in the way of sex education. It does not take long for the 17-year-old Meridian to prove to her mother and to herself that there are limits to how much or how little she is willing to sacrifice for her own child. From the beginning Meridian views Eddie Junior as a ball and chain. She amuses herself by fantasizing about ways to kill him—or herself. She soon does what her mother would consider unthinkable: she gives away her infant son. Mrs. Hill has raised six children without ever loving one; Meridian loves Eddie Junior enough, in an impersonal sort of way, to give him up: "One day she really looked at her child and loved him with as much love as she loved the moon or a tree, which was a considerable amount of impersonal love" (*Meridian*, 90). Unlike her mother and a long line of mothers before her, Meridian lives in an age of choice. She chooses a college education over the motherhood that she feels unsuited for, taking advantage of a scholarship to Saxon College.

The Failed Revolutionary

The move to Atlanta thrusts Meridian into the heart of the civil rights movement, but it does not provide a means of escape from the guilt that she feels for having failed as a daughter and as a mother. Because Saxon's young women are supposed to be as "pure as the driven snow," she has to deny her marriage, her divorce, and her motherhood. The guilt starts to affect her physically as she begins to lose her hair. She hears a voice, "a voice that cursed her existence—an existence that could not live up to the standard of motherhood that had gone before" (*Meridian*, 91). She also begins to have headaches—and a recurring nightmare in which she is a character in a novel whose existence presents a problem that will be solved only by her death. She comes as close to death as the living can come by occasionally slipping into a death-like trance. Her unspoken belief is that in giving up her physical existence, she can come closer to being pure spirit and thus more acceptable to her mother: "Meridian felt as if her body, growing frailer every day under the stress of her daily life, stood in the way of a reconciliation between her mother and that part of her own soul her mother could, perhaps, love. She valued her body less, because she hated its obstruction" (*Meridian*, 97). She almost dies before Miss Winter, a childless teacher at Saxon, yet a mother figure, saves her by granting her the forgiveness that her mother never could.

The scene is Meridian's room at Saxon, which she shares with Anne-Marion. Meridian, who has been in bed for a month before Anne-Marion seeks help, smiles up at Miss Winter out of her illness:

Now and again she saw clouds drift across Miss Winter's head and she amused herself picking out faces that she knew. When she slept she dreamed she was on a ship with her mother, and her mother was holding her over the railing about to drop her into the sea. Danger was all around and her mother refused to let her go.

"Mama, I *love* you. Let me go," she whispered, licking the salt from her mother's black arms.

Instinctively, as if Meridian were her own child, Miss Winter answered, close to her ear on the pillow, "I forgive you." (*Meridian*, 124–25)

Meridian does not take the symbolic plunge into the sea; she does not die. Her trances return occasionally, but Miss Winter's words start her back on the road to physical and mental health. She comes to see death in its relationship to life with the clear perspective of her childhood. Then too she had her trances, but they taught her the value of life over death, not the reverse.

Meridian's father made a living by teaching. His fulfillment in life, however, came from farming and from studying Native Americans, a people deprived of their heritage by the white man as fully as was the black man. His interests sprang from the fact that his small farm was part of an Indian burial ground, called the Sacred Serpent because of the shape of its raised mounds. (Walker reveals in "Eagle Rock" that the town where she was born had its own mound of stone eight feet high, raised by the Cherokees, that from above revealed the shape of an eagle [*Petunias*, 20–22].) The coil of the Sacred Serpent created a deep hollow with mysterious effects on those who entered it. There Meridian and her father both experienced the dizzying sensation of feeling spirit leave body and float free: "Her father said the Indians had constructed the coil in the Serpent's tail in order to give the living a sensation similar to that of dying: The body seemed to drop away, and only the spirit lived, set free in the world" (*Meridian*, 58).

Meridian was not convinced, however, that what was to be learned from the proximity to death was anything about dying: "It seemed to her that it was a way the living sought to expand the consciousness of being alive, there where the ground about them was filled with the dead" (*Meridian*, 59). Years later, in her dorm room at Saxon College, when Meridian is granted expiation for her sins against her biological mother by her symbolic mother, Miss Winter, Meridian chooses not to become pure spirit forever, but chooses rather a role among the living.

A similar choice confronts Meridian as she strives for years to define her role in the civil rights movement. Meridian's failure as a daughter and as a mother is only a part of the burden she bears. She also bears the burden of knowing that as a revolutionary she has failed. Anne-Marion and her other friends active in the civil rights movement turn on her when she cannot say that she would kill for the cause. Yes, she would die for the cause, but kill? To do so would be to destroy the world as she has known it. Meridian fears what the revolution will do to the art in her world. Thus she must define for herself the role of the artist in a time of revolution.

Unconcerned for her own physical existence, Meridian finds that the only times that she can forget her failures in her relationship with her mother are amidst the chaos and brutality of the activists' confrontations with police. She welcomes the beatings as though she deserves them, and in her mind she does. To have violence done to her seems justified; to return violence for violence, however, threatens the world as she has known it: "When she was transformed in church it was always by the purity of the singers' souls, which she could actually *hear*, the purity that lifted their songs like a flight of doves above her music-drunken head. If they committed murder—and to her even revolutionary murder was murder—*what would the music be like?*" (*Meridian*, 28).

A failure as Anne-Marion's type of revolutionary, ostracized by her friends in the North, Meridian returns to the South to live among the people, choosing life-giving—rather than life-destroying—means of supporting the revolution. After one child and one abortion, Meridian has her tubes tied, thereby removing the possibility of future children. Her mothering instincts surface, nonetheless, in the form her personal revolution takes.

The characteristic scene featuring Meridian, the quiet revolutionary, shows her leading a group of children. Such a scene opens the novel as Truman Held, her fellow civil rights worker and the father of her aborted child, follows her to a small town in Georgia. He watches bemused as she stares down the town's gaudy white tank, "bought during the sixties when the townspeople who were white felt under attack from 'outside agitators'—those members of the black community who thought equal rights for all should extend to blacks" (*Meridian*, 18). The right she fights for this time, on the children's behalf, is the simple right to see a freak show on a day other than that designated for blacks. The townsmen aim the old tank's gun at Meridian but ultimately are hesitant to shoot this strange lady in a conductor's cap, so this battle is quietly won.

Other battles that Meridian fights are for higher stakes, but always directly or indirectly for the children's benefit. A ditch that runs behind her house becomes a deathtrap for the neighborhood children, who do not know how to swim, when excess rain water is periodically drained from the local reservoir without warning. Meridian carries into a town meeting the decomposing and mangled body of the flood's latest victim, a five-year-old boy, and lays it beside the mayor's gavel. The mother who gave away her own son out of love now gives her love and protection to the children of strangers.

Even in Atlanta while attending Saxon, Meridian learned that the children are not always spared in times of revolution. She invited a young black girl to join a protest march, but that night heard the girl's screams echoing from another part of the jail. She tried to help the street urchin called Wild Child, who ate out of trash cans in the vicinity of Saxon, but lost her when the child, pregnant with a child of her own, was killed by a car.

Not all of the child victims of the 1960s' violence, however, are strangers to Meridian. One is the daughter produced by Truman's marriage to Lynne, a white exchange student who has come south in support of the movement. The climactic chapter of the novel, "Camara," is named after this little girl beaten to death in a savage attack.

Sometime after she follows Martin Luther King, Jr., the epitome of nonviolent revolutionaries, to his grave, in a church scene in "Camara" that recalls the earlier scene in which she lost her mother, Meridian is finally able to find her own place in the revolution. The change in the music is one clue that the church she happens into one Sunday morning is not the same church she attended as a child. This church does not preach meek acceptance of death—the resignation resonant in her father's singing voice. This rather is the church militant and its music the music of war: "'Let the martial songs be written,' she found herself quoting Margaret Walker's famous poem; 'let the dirges disappear!' She started and looked quickly around her. The people looked exactly as they had ever since she had known black churchgoing people, which was all her life, but they had changed the music! She was shocked" (*Meridian*, 195).

The sermon, too, is different. In the voice of King, the preacher launches into an attack on "Tricky Dick" Nixon. The agenda he has in mind for his congregation is very much of this world, not the next:

He looked down on the young men in the audience and forbade them to participate in the Vietnam war. He told the young women to stop looking for husbands and try to get something useful in their heads. He told the older congregants that they should be ashamed of the way they let their young children fight their battles for them. He told them they were cowardly and pathetic when they sent their small children alone into white neighborhoods to go to school. He abused the black teachers present who did not, he said, work hard enough to teach black youth because they obviously had no faith in them. . . . God was not mentioned, except as a reference. (*Meridian*, 195–96)

Meridian glances up to see that the usual stained-glass Christ holding a lamb has been replaced with a tall, broad-shouldered black man (B. B. King) with a guitar in one hand and a sword dripping with blood in the other.

The service on this particular Sunday is to commemorate the death of a young man martyred in the fight for civil rights. The martyr's father stands before the congregation, red-eyed and unable to speak except for three simple words, "My son died."

The service over, Meridian ponders the vague love she feels for this young man who gave his life for the cause, but wonders what good her love or her grief can do one already dead. As she asks that question, she comes to realize the significance of the ceremony that she has just witnessed:

The people in the church were saying to the red-eyed man that his son had not died for nothing, and that if his son should come again they would protect his life with their own. . . . [They were saying,] "If you will let us weave your story and your son's life and death into what we already know—into the songs, the sermons, the 'brother and sister'—we will soon be so angry we cannot help but move. Understand this," they were saying, "the church (and Meridian knew they did not mean simply 'church,' as in Baptist, Methodist or what not, but rather communal spirit, togetherness, righteous convergence), the music, the form of worship that has always sustained us, the kind of ritual you share with us, these are the ways to transformation that we know. We want to take this with us as far as we can."

In comprehending this, there was in Meridian's chest a breaking as if a tight string binding her lungs had given way, allowing her to breathe freely. For she understood, finally, that the respect she owed her life was to continue, against whatever obstacles, to live it, and not to give up any particle of it without a fight to the death, preferably *not* her own. . . . Under a large tree beside the road, crowded now with the cars returning from church, she made a promise to the red-eyed man herself: that yes, indeed, she *would* kill, before she allowed anyone to murder his son again. (*Meridian,* 199–200)

The chapter's title, "Camara," implies that she would also kill before she would let anyone murder Camara again.

In the *Revolutionary Petunias* poem "The QPP," Walker also writes of the quietly pacifist peaceful but acknowledges there comes a time when even the peaceful pacifist chooses to kill rather than be killed.

Meridian, however, is destined to be one of those who only stand and wait to bear arms in defense of a cause. Her dedication to the promise made the red-eyed man weakens occasionally, but she has discovered her true role in the revolution.

> I have been allowed to see how the new capacity to do anything, including kill, for our freedom—beyond sporadic acts of violence—is to emerge, and flower, but I am not yet at the point of being able to kill anyone myself, nor—except for the false urgings that come to me in periods of grief and rage—will I ever be. I am a failure then, as the kind of revolutionary Anne-Marion and her acquaintances were. . . .
>
> It was this, Meridian thought, I have not wanted to face, this that has caused me to suffer: I am not to belong to the future. I am to be left, listening to the old music, beside the highway. But then, she thought, perhaps it will be my part to walk behind the real revolutionaries—those who know they must spill blood in order to help the poor and the black and therefore go right ahead—and when they stop to wash off the blood and find their throats too choked with the smell of murdered flesh to sing, I will come forward and sing from memory songs they will need once more to hear. For it is the song of the people, transformed by the experiences of each generation, that holds them together, and if any part of it is lost the people suffer and are without soul. If I can only do that, my role will not have been a useless one after all. (*Meridian*, 201)

Walker captures the same idea in a quotation from Albert Camus with which she opens the title section of *Revolutionary Petunias*: "Beauty, no doubt, does not make revolutions. But a day will come when revolutions will have need of beauty" (*Petunias*, 28).

Some of Meridian's "songs" constitute the next three chapters of *Meridian*—"Travels," "Treasure," and "Pilgrimage." The book ends as it began, showing Meridian going about the rural South, trying to persuade blacks to register to vote and offering them whatever help she can regardless of whether they choose to register.

Meridian still wears the conductor's cap to hide her thinning hair, but now the hair is growing back: she is returning to health, both physically and mentally. Each of her "performances" for the good of the people is followed by one of her fainting spells. She gradually brings her body out of its paralysis, though, crawls out of her sleeping bag (one of her few remaining material possessions), and faces life. Truman compares her to Lazarus, but feels the analogy is not wholly accurate because Lazarus needed help in bringing himself back to life; Meridian is strong enough to do it alone. At the end of the novel Truman watches her crawl out of the sleeping bag for the last time.

She has chosen to refuse death: "'The only new thing now,' she had said to herself, . . . 'would be the refusal of Christ to accept crucifixion. King . . . should have refused. Malcolm, too, should have refused. All those characters in all those novels that require death to end the book should refuse. All saints should walk away. Do their bit, then—just walk away'" (*Meridian*, 151). Meridian does what she would have the saints and martyrs do: she just walks away.

When Meridian agonized over her role in the revolution well into the 1970s, Truman told her that no one was asking such questions anymore, that revolution, like so much else, had proven to be a passing fad. When Meridian rises from her sleeping bag for the last time, however, in the final scene in the novel, Truman takes her place there. This time it is Truman who is dizzy, Truman who puts on the conductor's cap Meridian has finally left behind. He wonders "if Meridian knew that the sentence of bearing the conflict in her own soul which she had imposed on herself—and lived through—must now be borne in terror by all the rest of them" (*Meridian*, 220).

Revolutionaries and Lovers

The "rest of them" in this novel are most significantly Truman and his white wife, Lynne. Meridian's story confronts the question of whether art can survive in time of revolution; Truman and Lynne's asks whether love can. Similarly, Walker introduces the poems in *Revolutionary Petunias* as poems about revolutionaries but also about lovers. In that sense, then, parallels are found between the collection of poetry and *Meridian*. In the poem "Lost My Voice? Of Course." a childhood bully tells Walker the revolution cannot afford poems about love and flowers. Yet poems of love set in time of revolution may well be about flowers—about revolutionary petunias and the people who are incorrect enough to want to nurture those petunias. Truman and Lynne are "incorrect," of course, according to society's standards, because of their interracial marriage. While Meridian's story ends on an optimistic note, however, Truman and Lynne's relationship, like those in some of the poems in *Revolutionary Petunias*, suffers from an inability to expand in love (*Petunias*, epigraph).

Walker herself married Mel Leventhal when in Mississippi an interracial couple could not live together legally. She dedicates "While Love Is Unfashionable" to him and in the poem proposes that they dare to walk bareheaded and gather blossoms under fire. In marrying during the heat of the 1960s' civil rights movement, Truman and Lynne dare to gather blossoms under fire. The love they profess for one another is certainly "unfashionable" and one of the "Forbidden Things" of the poem by that name in *Revolutionary Petunias*. The full extent of the danger their love places them in is brought sharply home to Truman when the "fire" under which he and Lynne have been gathering blossoms turns into real bullets aimed at Truman and their friend and fellow civil rights worker Tommy Odds. When Tommy loses part of his arm after being shot leaving a strategy meeting, guilt and the need for expiation replace compassion and trust as the controlling force in the relationship between Lynne and Truman.

Truman tries to understand in what sense Lynne could be guilty for what Tommy has suffered. On a literal level she is "guilty" of having been seen in public with the two black men. In a more general sense, she is guilty of being white, of being a white woman, and, as Truman puts it, "of being, period" (*Meridian*, 135). The trust that she has gradually built among members of the black community starts to erode as the movement experiences a shift toward violence.

Later Lynne tries to expiate her guilt by letting Tommy "rape" her: "As he said, it wasn't really rape. She had not screamed once, or even struggled much. To her, it was worse than rape because she felt circumstances had not permitted her to scream" (*Meridian*, 158). In the split second that she knows she could break free, she also knows why she won't: "There was a moment when she knew she could force him from her. But it was a flash. She lay instead thinking of his feelings, his hardships, of the way he was black and belonged to people who lived without hope; she thought about the loss of his arm. She felt her own guilt" (*Meridian*, 159). She doesn't struggle, then, and afterward, she kisses his stump and forgives him.

In the ensuing showdown between Truman and Tommy (the fact that the scene is printed in italics implies that perhaps we are not to believe that such an event ever took place) Tommy accuses Lynne of having married Truman out of the same sort of pity. Tommy scoffs at Truman's suggestion that Lynne felt sorry for him because of his arm. Tommy recognizes Lynne's true motives—he knows she pities him because he is black—and also knows that Lynne initially became involved with Truman because he was black, thus exotic and forbidden to a Jewish girl from New Jersey.

In anger, as the marriage falls apart, Lynne sees their relationship from the opposite perspective and accuses Truman of having married her as a revolutionary act: "You only married me because you were too much of a coward to throw a bomb at all the crackers who make you sick. You're like the rest of those nigger zombies. No life of your own at all unless it's something against white folks" (*Meridian,* 149).

Lynne and Truman's last chance to expand in love is their daughter Camara, but her death destroys the last thing that held them together. Lynne feels a certain generosity in believing that she is freeing Truman to go back "to his own." She assumes, incorrectly, that he will return to Meridian. He instead finds another white lover, but he does, in a sense, always return to Meridian. By this time, Meridian has forgiven Truman for not loving her, for loving a white woman at the very time she herself was carrying his black baby. The feeling that she has left for him is not sexual, but a sisterly sort of caring. It is the same sort of brotherly/sisterly love that is all Truman can offer Lynne near the end of the novel in a chapter called "Atonement: Later, in the Same Life."

This whole air of forgiveness and brotherly/sisterly love permeates the novel's end, just as an air of guilt permeates the rest of it. Near the end, Meridian writes two poems. One of them begins thus:

> i want to put an end to guilt
> i want to put and [*sic*] end to shame
> whatever you have done my sister
> (my brother)
> know i wish to forgive you
> love you (*Meridian,* 213)

The poems, the songs, the stories—these are the links between individuals and between generations, as Meridian learned earlier. Another glimmer of hope for the future links her with a storyteller from Saxon's past. An elderly slave woman on the plantation that became Saxon College once told a gruesome story in such vivid detail that the heart of one of the family's young sons failed him and he died. The slave was punished by having her tongue cut out. She saved the tongue, though, and planted it under a scrawny magnolia that later flourished to become the famous Sojourner, focal point of the Saxon campus—until the Saxon students cut it down as an act of protest. Anne-Marion's last letter to Meridian contains a picture of the vast trunk of the Sojourner with a tiny shoot of new life growing out of one side.

The Sojourner, a living memorial to an uneducated artist, did not die. Neither does the petunia, a living memorial to the rebel in each individual. In the last poem in *Revolutionary Petunias*, "The Nature of This Flower Is to Bloom," the revolutionary petunia is hailed as enduring in all its glorious color for itself and for those who look upon it with deserving eyes.

Chapter Six

Beautiful, Whole, and Free:
You Can't Keep a Good Woman Down

Walker ends *In Search of Our Mothers' Gardens* with a positive image of dancing. In the concluding paragraph of the last essay, "Beauty: When the Other Dancer Is the Self," Walker dreams that her two "selves" are dancing with one another. One part of her has dreaded the day when her daughter will discover the scar on her mother's eye that Walker has borne since age eight; this is the self that cringes when she sees her daughter focusing on the eye and braces for childhood's cruel response to physical differences. The other self is a part of her that Walker felt died with the BB shot to her eye that left both the scar and the shame of feeling suddenly ugly and disfigured.

Walker tells us that a great deal of the pain that she had suffered for 20 years left when her daughter saw not a disfiguring scar but rather a world in her eye. In the dream that comes to her that night, Walker is as happy as she has ever been, and she is joined in her joyous dancing by "another bright-faced dancer": "We dance and kiss each other and hold each other through the night. The other dancer has obviously come through all right, as I have done. She is beautiful, whole and free. And she is also me" (*Gardens,* 393).

You Can't Keep a Good Woman Down, Walker's 1981 collection of short stories, explores the hidden beautiful, whole, and free selves that her fictional black women discover or rediscover when they, like Grange Copeland, realize that definition of self must come from within. In the last story in the collection, "Source," one character tells another, "Your dilemma was obvious. You, even *objectively* speaking, did not know who you were. What you were going to do next; which 'you' would be the one to survive" (166). More often in this collection than in Walker's earlier volumes, the self that survives is not a self dictated by others.

The women of this volume continue the progress toward spiritual health and self-definition begun by Ruth in *The Third Life of Grange Copeland* and Meridian Hill in *Meridian*. That this collection is Walker's celebration of women's fighting spirit, in contrast to *In Love and Trouble*'s portrayal of their vulnerability, is reflected in its title and in the quotation from Hermann Hesse that serves as its epigraph:

> It is harder to kill something
> that is spiritually alive
> than it is to bring the dead
> back to life.

Meridian goes through a symbolic resurrection once she realizes that her duty to her own life is to live it even if that means literally fighting for her life. The women of *You Can't Keep a Good Woman Down* join her in fighting for their spiritual and emotional lives.

The Eve of Becoming

The issue of self-definition is illustrated most forcefully in "The Abortion." Like Walker, the main character, Imani, has an abortion while in college. Looking back, she sometimes recalls the experience as a freeing one, "bearing as it had all the marks of a supreme coming of age and a seizing of the direction of her own life" (*GW*, 67). Seven years later, Imani is now married and the mother of a two-year-old daughter, Clarice. When she finds herself pregnant once again, abortion is legal—also cheaper, safer, quicker, and supposedly less painful—but she realizes that she is "still not in control of her sensuality, and only through violence and with money (for the flight, for the operation itself) in control of her body" (*GW*, 69). When she boards a plane, alone, to fly from her small Southern town to New York for the abortion, she bristles at her husband Clarence's whispered "Take care of yourself." She not only resents his not going along to take care of her—his presence back home is essential to the success of the town's new black mayor—but she also resents equally her self-pitying need to be taken care of.

The turning point comes for Imani when, back from New York, she sits in her rocker with Clarice dozing on her lap and Clarence resting his head against her knees: "She felt he was asking for nurture when she needed it herself. She felt the two of them, Clarence and Clarice, clinging to her, using her. And that the only way she could claim herself, feel herself distinct from them, was by doing something painful, self-defining but self-destructive." When she can no longer stand the pressure of Clarence's head, she tells him, "Have a vasectomy or stay in the guest room. Nothing is going to touch me anymore that isn't harmless" (GW, 71).

Clarence does as Imani wishes. He has a vasectomy, but it comes too late. Their marriage ends for Imani the day after the abortion when, still weak from the surgery, she goes to the yearly memorial service for Holly Monroe, a young black woman shot down on the way home from her high school graduation five years earlier. Sitting in the stifling heat of the church, the pain in her uterus increasing, Imani realizes that in a sense Holly Monroe was every young black girl. "And an even deeper truth was that Holly Monroe was herself. Herself shot down, aborted on the eve of becoming herself" (GW, 73). She also realizes that Clarence has lingered in the vestibule to talk politics with the mayor. When she tiptoes to the church door to hiss that their voices are carrying into the church, the two men merely turn and walk outside to finish their conversation. For two more years Imani goes through the motions of marriage, but ultimately she has to complete the painful but self-defining separation begun on the night she returned from New York, a separation that becomes inevitable when her husband turns and walks away from Holly Monroe's memorial service: "From that moment in the heat at the church door, she had uncoupled herself from him, in a separation that made him, except occasionally, little more than a stranger. . . . She had known the moment she left the marriage, the exact second," but on Clarence, the moment had left "no perceptible mark" (GW, 75–76).

Imani, unlike some of Walker's earlier fictional women, does not cling to her loyalty to her black man to the point of total self-abnegation or self-destruction. She acknowledges her marriage for the fraud that it is and knows that she must be the one to walk away from it because ultimately Clarence is willing to settle for fraud and she is not.

"The Lover" also features a fraudulent marriage but adds a newfound sexual freedom that provides escape from an unfulfilling marriage. The unnamed main character of this story gives her husband a child as a gift because she likes and admires him. Theirs has been from the beginning a rather passionless marriage, at most a sexually comfortable one, and after their child is born, she stops thinking of her husband sexually at all. She views the child as a temporary distraction in her life but looks forward to the day that it will go off to boarding school, leaving her free once again. In the meantime, she enters into a brief affair with a fellow writer during the two months of temporary freedom she finds at a New England artists' colony, more in a spirit of adventure than out of any sense of need: "When she had first seen him she had thought . . . 'my lover,' and had liked, deep down inside, the illicit sound of it. She had never had a lover; he would be her first. Afterwards, she would be truly a woman of her time" (*GW*, 34).

This Walker creation is a woman in love with the sensation of being in love, as she tries to explain to her uncomprehending lover, Ellis, whom Walker describes as "a professional lover of mainly older women artists who came to the Colony every year to work and play" (*GW*, 36). She is coldly dispassionate about everything else—her child, her husband, her writing, and even Ellis. The idea of being in love is physically exciting to her in a way that even her lovemaking with Ellis is not. That is disappointing at best, "but it hardly mattered, since what mattered was the fact of having a lover" (*GW*, 37). It is quite clear by the end of the story that she will have others, one of whom could even be her own husband if she could have sex with him in the same spirit of adventure with which she looks forward to a whole series of future lovers: "At night, after a rousing but unsatisfactory evening with Ellis, she dreamed of her husband making love to her on the kitchen floor at home, where the sunlight collected in a pool beneath the window, and lay in bed next day dreaming of all the faraway countries, daring adventures, passionate lovers still to be found" (*GW*, 39). She has discovered in herself a sensuality that has lain dormant in her since her college days. When Ellis first approaches her and saves her from a boring conversation with an aging poet with the question "Have you been waiting long?" it "suddenly occurred to her that indeed she had" (*GW*, 33).

Coming Together

Two stories in the collection deal with the threat that pornography poses to relationships between black men and women. One called simply "Porn" shows a successful sexual relationship destroyed by pornography. The other, less effective as fiction, "Coming Apart: By Way of Introduction to Lorde, Teish and Gardner," records one woman's fight against the dehumanizing effects of pornography. Both show that the dignity of the black woman need not be sacrificed to the black male's views on sexuality.

The man and woman in "Porn" have an almost perfect sexual relationship. Unlike that of the married couple in "The Lover," their relationship is built on sexual passion. The beginning of the end comes for them when they try to make an almost perfect sexual arrangement perfect by trying to achieve simultaneous orgasm. To that end, the man draws out his pornography collection and tries to interest the woman in it.

The point, of course, is for her to be aroused by what arouses him. She is not. In fact, once she has had a glimpse of the world of his fantasies, the continued success of their relationship depends on her being able to forget what she has glimpsed: "The long-term accommodation that protects marriage and other such relationships is, she knows, forgetfulness. She will forget what turns him on" (GW, 81). But she cannot. When they make love again, she attempts to place herself mentally in the scenes graphically presented in his magazines, but she doesn't fit, and nothing in the attempt excites or stimulates her. He, on the other hand, has to fantasize in order to be able to make love to her successfully. Now when he tries to slip her into the roles from the magazines, his frantic attempt fails. What frightens him most is that she might open her eyes and look at him totally objectively. To do so would break the spell. But the spell is already broken. When she holds him the last time they make love, she does so nostalgically, saying good-bye silently to what they once had, as "he feels himself sliding down the wall that is her body, and expelled from inside her" (GW, 84).

This woman shares with the wife in "Coming Apart" the knowledge that when her man makes love to her, it is not really her, but some fantasized version of her drawn from his pornographic magazines. Each responds in an infinitely more positive way than did the wife in Walker's "Her Sweet Jerome," who committed suicide when she discovered that she had a print "rival." Each of these later, healthier Walker women refuses to have her sexual identity defined by a man's sexist or racist fantasies.

When the wife in "Coming Apart" finds her husband's *Jiveboy* with its nude blondes and brunettes, he protests that they mean nothing, but she thinks, "But they are not me, those women. She cannot say she is jealous of pictures on a page. That she feels invisible. Rejected. Overlooked. She says instead, to herself: He is right. I will grow up.

Adjust. Swim with the tide" (*GW,* 43). Even more distressing than the mere existence of his fantasy world, however, is its racist roots and his continuation of that racist past. It is no better when he brings home *Jivers,* "a black magazine, filled with bronze and honey-colored women," because in its pages black women are portrayed as less than human.

When she studies her own brown and black body in the mirror, in her imagination she sees it age into her mother's, yet is surprised to find that she considers her mother, even late in life, very sexy. Reminded thus of a wider range of human sexuality than pornography accommodates, she resolves not to "grow up," not to "adjust," but to fight to change her husband's demeaning and limiting perceptions of black women.

"Coming Apart" proves that Walker is least successful as a fiction writer when she lets devotion to a cause outweigh plot and characterization. Her motives, at least, are worthy ones. In the introduction to the piece, she writes, "I believe it is only by writing stories in which pornography is confronted openly and explicitly that writers can make a contribution, in their own medium, to a necessary fight" (*GW,* 42). The history of the piece explains some of its weaknesses as fiction. "Coming Apart" was originally written as an introduction to a chapter of a book on pornography called *Take Back the Night* edited by Laura Lederer. Although it was eventually printed in the volume as a story rather than as the introduction to the essays by Audre Lorde, Luisah Teish, and Tracey A. Gardner for which it was intended, it does not work quite as well as a story as Walker hoped. She acknowledges that she would have treated the material differently had it been written as a story originally. Her "Introduction" appeared in *Ms.* as "A Fable" before *Take Back the Night* was published.

This fable of one woman's attempt to reform her husband's misguided thinking is a loose vehicle used to present Lorde, Teish, and Gardner's views on pornography. Quotes from the three become the ammunition in the battle for respect that the wife wages against her husband. When she quotes to him from Audre Lorde on the use and abuse of feelings, he knows that their relationship has changed: "He realized he can never have her again sexually the way he has had her since their second year of marriage, as though her body belonged to someone else. He sees, down the road, the dissolution of the marriage, a constant search for more perfect bodies, or dumber wives" (*GW,* 46).

The moral of the fable, however, is not that the secret to happiness is to marry dumber wives. Rather the moral is that the husband must come to know himself in all of his prejudice before he can know his wife again in any sense of the word. His wife erodes his resistance by reading to him nightly from her feminist "sisters." His conversion is as predictable as it is idealistic. What she makes him see about himself, with the help of Lorde, Teish, and Gardner, is that as a result of first the civil rights movement and then the black power movement—in neither of which he was actively involved—he feels he has progressed beyond her into a white world that has always, in its thinking about black women, associated sex with violence, that in accepting pornography used against black women, "he has detached himself from his own blackness in attempting to identify black women only by their sex" (GW, 48).

He might have continued making love to a fantasy had he not revealed to his wife the roots of that fantasy in the violence and dehumanization of slavery. "Still, he does not know how to make love without the fantasies fed to him by movies and magazines (whose characters' pursuits are irrelevant or antithetical to his concerns) that have insinuated themselves between him and his wife, so that the totality of her body, her entire corporeal reality is alien to him. Even to clutch her in lust is automatically to shut his eyes. Shut his eyes, and . . . he chuckles bitterly . . . dream of England" (GW, 53).

In an ending no more believable than the endings of the fables after which the story is modeled, the couple decide they need some time apart. In his loneliness, the man turns to his magazines once again and then to his wife's books, and "when she returns, it is sixty percent *her* body that he moves against in the sun, her own black skin affirmed in the brightness of his eyes" (GW, 53). He is no longer dreaming either of England or of any other woman, black or white, but is looking at his wife in her own dark beauty. Their relationship has survived, and supposedly been strengthened by, the sort of objective scrutiny that destroyed the one in "Porn."

Fighting Mad

Another of Walker's fighters is the narrator of "How Did I Get Away with Killing One of the Biggest Lawyers in the State? It Was Easy." Because she is a poor black teenager with a mother who works as a maid and a father she never knew, she is not a born fighter; her first response to violence or injustice is not to fight, but to acquiesce. She is raped at age 12 but shrugs it off with "I never told anybody. For, what could they do?" (*GW*, 23). When she is 14 and the prominent white lawyer her mother works for tricks her into his car, drives her to his office, and rapes her, she again tells no one, but two days later, she willingly gets into his car again. He is at least clean, and he gives her money and gifts. They "keep going together" for two years, even after her mother finds out and, appalled, points out, in details suspiciously reminiscent of George Wallace, the truth of how his people view hers:

"That night she told me something I hadn't paid much attention to before. She said: 'On top of everything else, that man's daddy goes on the t.v. every night and says folks like us ain't even human.' It was his daddy who had stood in the schoolhouse door saying it would be over his dead body before any black children would come into a white school.

"But do you think that stopped me? No. . . . What did I know about 'equal rights'? What did I care about 'integration'? I was 16! I wanted somebody to tell me I was pretty, and he was telling me that all the time. I even thought it was *brave* of him to go with me. History? What did I know about History?" (*GW*, 24–25)

The lawyer, Bubba, persuades her to have her mother committed to an insane asylum, and three months later her mother really is insane. Waking up to reality, the narrator tries unsuccessfully to get Bubba to help her have her mother released, but he refuses. Even after that, she continues to see him—"out of habit, I guess"—until her mother dies and she coldly, with no remorse, takes Bubba's gun from his desk drawer and kills him. During the funeral she sits on Bubba's wife's bed, where she and Bubba have made love for years, babysitting for his children and eating fried chicken the widow made. The money she stole from Bubba's safe will guarantee her the college education he always promised her.

Still another fighter is the title character of the story "Elethia," which Walker has called her creative solution to one problem that typified the racism that existed in her hometown of Eatonton, Georgia. There was "until a few years ago" an Uncle Remus Restaurant in Eatonton—for whites only, of course—which featured in its window a dummy of a black man, "an elderly, kindly, cottony-haired darkie, seated in a rocking chair" (*Living,* 31). Walker fantasized about liberating him, "using Army tanks and guns." Through the character Elethia, she does free Uncle Albert, her fictional counterpart of the Uncle Remus dummy.

Working one summer as a salad girl in the restaurant where the grinning Uncle Albert decorates the window, Elethia discovers that he is not a dummy but rather a real stuffed man. His intense smile with its shining false teeth belies the brutality of the life that he led as a slave—"All them teeth. Hell, all Albert's teeth was knocked out before he was grown"—and his pose of willing servitude belies the fact that he refused ever to work in "the big house"—"always broke up stuff" (*GW,* 30).

One night Elethia and her friends steal Uncle Albert and burn him in the high school incinerator, each keeping a bottle of his ashes. Their act of rebellion leaves Elethia glancing back over her shoulder at the slightest noise, the seemingly solid foundations of her life shaken, yet she feels that in burning the corpse, they were doing what Albert Porter would have wanted. She goes to college, and her friends join the army, where they learn "skills that would get them through more than a plate glass window" (*GW,* 30). They discover Uncle Alberts all over the world, including in Elethia's textbooks. "Everywhere she looked there was an Uncle Albert (and many Aunt Albertas, it goes without saying). But she had her jar of ashes, the old-timers' memories [of Albert] written down. . . . And she was careful that, no matter how compelling the hype, Uncle Alberts, in her own mind, were not permitted to exist" (*GW,* 30).

These Walker women are ones who act rather than acquiesce.

Whole and Free

In Walker's earlier collection, *In Love and Trouble,* one of the few women who exhibit spiritual health is the narrator of "Everyday Use," perhaps the most often anthologized of all Walker's short stories. The story seems oddly out of place in a volume about the suffering caused by misplaced loyalty to black men, because Mrs. Johnson manages quite well without a man and seems more at peace with herself than the vast majority of early Walker women. Yet Mrs. Johnson exists in the story as a foil for her daughter Dee, who, like other women in *In Love and Trouble,* suffers from misplaced loyalties or, perhaps more accurately in her case, misplaced priorities, although Dee remains blind to the falsity and shallowness of the life she lives as a modern young black woman.

Dee makes the mistake of believing that one's heritage is something that one puts on display if and when such a display is fashionable. The very name that she prefers, Wangero Leewanika Kemanjo, is one "put on" to replace the one passed down to her through generations of Johnson women. Dee has taken on a fashionable African name, fashionable African clothing and hairstyles, a fashionable Muslim boyfriend, and a fashionable desire to show off the primitive lifestyle of those whose name she rejects. When Dee comes home to visit her mother and her sister Maggie, she takes photographs of them, being careful to capture in the background her mother's three-room house with no real windows but rather with jagged holes cut in the sides and covered with shutters secured only with rawhide. Dee and her boyfriend exchange knowing glances that reveal that they perceive Dee's mother as a quaint yet entertaining artifact.

Dee wants to take home with her some bits and pieces of her heritage. She wants the churn top to make into a centerpiece for her alcove table and the dasher for "something artistic." She never stops to consider that these pieces of "art" are also useful. They are valuable to Dee because they are old and vaguely connected with members of her family now dead and gone. When Maggie quietly speaks up to explain the family history behind the churn, it is clear that, for her, heritage is more than art. Maggie, badly burned in the fire that claimed the Johnsons' previous house, has never gone out into the world as Dee has, but she lives her heritage every day. Even a churn handle, priceless because it bears the handprints of generations of Johnsons, can still be used to make butter. Such simple arts are the stuff of Maggie's daily life.

If Walker's portrayal of Dee draws her story into line with the others in *In Love and Trouble* because of her easy vulnerability to the fad of the moment, which gives a false and shallow picture of who she is, both as a black woman and as a member of the Johnson family, her mother is more at home with the women of *You Can't Keep a Good Woman Down*. In both size and spirit she is linked most directly with Gracie Mae Still, the main character of "Nineteen Fifty-Five," which opens the later volume.

Mrs. Johnson is Walker's introduction to the type of androgynous figure that in *The Color Purple* strikes a successful balance between male and female. In spite of her dream of appearing svelte and smooth talking on a late night talk show, Mrs. Johnson accepts the reality of her existence, and her pride in her strength comes through in her description of herself:

> In real life I am a large, big-boned woman with rough, man-working hands. In the winter I wear flannel nightgowns to bed and overalls during the day. I can kill and clean a hog as mercilessly as a man. My fat keeps me hot in zero weather. I can work outside all day, breaking ice to get water for washing; I can eat pork liver cooked over the open fire minutes after it comes steaming from the hog. One winter I knocked a bull calf straight in the brain between the eyes with a sledge hammer and had the meat hung up to chill before nightfall. But of course all this does not show on television. (*Trouble,* 48)

Although Dee finds her mother and sister woefully backward and ignorant, the knowledge of the outside world Dee tries to force on them is knowledge they probably do not need. Mrs. Johnson can take an objective look at who and what she is and find not disillusionment but an easy satisfaction. Simple pleasures—a dip of snuff, a cooling breeze across a clean swept yard, church songs, the soothing movements of milk cows—are enough. In her dreams she may be someone else, but she realizes that phantom self for the fantasy that it is.

Gracie Mae Still shares with Mrs. Johnson a sense of health and wholeness; with Gracie Mae, it is the health and wholeness that come with being an artist whose works are outpourings of honest emotion. In a 1981 interview with Kay Bonetti, Walker discussed her envy of musicians, who "can put so much of themselves into what they sing. There's nothing between what they feel and what they say, if it's really good, and I like that . . . because it means a type of freedom for them."[1]

Gracie Mae has written songs that have been the envy of such greats as Bessie Smith, but her music is successful only when Traynor, a young man described in terms that make him sound suspiciously like Elvis Presley, records one of her songs. Walker leaves it up to her readers to draw any parallels between Elvis and Traynor, preferring to view Traynor as a more general symbol of white exploitation of black music. Traynor is a pitiable character, however, because he cannot understand the songs that he sings. He is trying to sing something that he lacks the experience to sing or to interpret. He says of Gracie Mae's song:

> I done sung that song seem like a million times this year. . . . I sung it on the Grand Ole Opry, I sung it on the Ed Sullivan show. I sung it on Mike

Douglas, I sung it at the Cotton Bowl, the Orange Bowl. I sung it at Festivals. I sung it at Fairs. I sung it overseas in Rome, Italy, and once in a submarine *underseas*. I've sung it and sung it, and I'm making forty thousand dollars a day offa it, and you know what, I don't have the faintest notion what that song means. (*GW*, 8)

In "Everyday Use" art, when it is more than simply a fad, is inextricably bound up with life. Traynor is a commerical success as an artist, the latest fad on the rock-and-roll scene, yet he is a spiritual failure because for him the link between art and life is never forged. Traynor has no more understanding of life than he has of the songs he is famous for. He tells Gracie Mae, "I married but it never went like it was supposed to. I never could squeeze any of my own life either into it or out of it. It was like singing somebody else's record. I copied the way it was sposed to be *exactly* but I never had a clue what marriage meant" (*GW*, 13). His lack of understanding reaches its broadest implications when Gracie Mae dreams that Traynor has just split up with his fifteenth wife and he says, "*You meet 'em for no reason. You date 'em for no reason. I do it all but I swear it's just like somebody else doing it. I feel like I can't remember Life*" (*GW*, 19). Of his own music, he writes to Gracie Mae, "*I've been thinking about writing some songs of my own but every time I finish one it don't seem to be about nothing I've actually lived myself. . . . Everybody still loves that song of yours. They ask me all the time what do I think it means, really. I mean, they want to know just what I want to know. Where out of your life did it come from?*" (*GW*, 11).

Gracie Mae achieved her understanding of both art and life by way of suffering. Her audience may have been small compared to Traynor's, but as she explains to him, "It would have been worth my life to try to sing 'em somebody else's stuff that I didn't know nothing about" and "Couldn't be nothing worse than being famous the world over for something you don't even understand" (*GW*, 17, 14). The aging Gracie Mae knows even more about life than did the young one. She knows that much of what she wrote early was a bluff, but she explains, "The trick is to live long enough to put your young bluffs to use. Now if I was to sing that song today I'd tear it up. 'Cause I done lived long enough to know it's *true*. Them words could hold me up." Traynor responds, "I ain't lived that long" (*GW*, 14).

Walker contends that white America has not lived long enough either. In her interview with Bonetti, Walker says, "Whites are going to have to go through a whole lot to be able to sing, but that's what

singing is, I think—having to go through a lot, understand a lot, and
suffer a lot." Art, on the other hand, helps some fortunate individuals
through the suffering: "One of the functions of art really is to help you
grow, to help you become whole, and to help you become a better
person, and if it doesn't do that, I think you should plant peanuts or
something" (Bonetti). Traynor might have been happier planting peanuts. Through her music, though, Gracie Mae has found a type of
freedom that all of Traynor's fame and money cannot buy. Part of her
freedom is the freedom to be her content if overweight self. She occasionally diets, but at one point she concludes, "I'll never seen three
hundred pounds again. . . . I got to thinking about it one day an' I
thought: aside from the fact that they say it's unhealthy, my fat ain't
never been no trouble. Mens always have loved me. My kids ain't never
complained. Plus they's fat. And fat like I is I looks distinguished. You
see me coming and know somebody's *there*" (*GW*, 12). Gracie Mae may
be unhealthy physically because of her fat, but she is spiritually as
healthy and whole as they come.

Chapter Seven

Letters to God:
The Color Purple

Walker's third novel, *The Color Purple* (1982), won both the Pulitzer Prize and the American Book Award for Fiction. The novel won increased fame—and notoriety—in 1985 with the release of the film adaptation, directed by Steven Spielberg, known for such blockbusters as *E.T.* and *Close Encounters of the Third Kind.* After some initial reservations—she didn't even know who Spielberg was—Walker eventually concluded, with a wisecrack to her daughter Rebecca, "Well, maybe if he can do Martians, he can do us."[1] Quincy Jones, one of Spielberg's coproducers and responsible for the film's music, convinced her that he would ensure that neither they nor their race would be embarrassed, and Walker went off to the country to try her hand at writing the screenplay. Three months later she gave up, and the job in time went to Dutchman Menno Meyjes, who had the disadvantages of being white and male, but brought to his treatment of the characters' nonstandard dialect a background of having grown up in a part of Holland where the folk dialect was looked down upon by those who spoke standard Dutch (Dworkin, 68, 70).

The movie opens with a shot of two young black girls romping through a vast field of purple flowers. It soon becomes obvious, however, that one is hampered, young as she is, by the heaviness of pregnancy. Celie, the pregnant 14-year-old of this opening scene and the main character of the novel, is based on Walker's great-great-grandmother, who was raped and impregnated at age 11 by her master, Walker's great-great-grandfather. The fact that Celie's rapist is black—is in fact the man whom she believes to be her father (he is much later found to be her stepfather instead)—was one of the reasons that both the novel and the movie brought an angry outcry from some segments of the black community. The argument was that in spite of the fact that by contractual agreement at least half of the people working off-screen on the movie would be "women or blacks or Third World people" (Dworkin, 70), onscreen there appeared not a single positive black male role model, and the portrayal of black family life was, at best, demeaning.

In the novel, when Celie's mother becomes too ill and too worn out from childbearing to satisfy her husband's sexual appetite, he rapes Celie repeatedly and then sells or gives away the two children born of his sin. Celie is left wondering whether he has perhaps even murdered them. She is also left unable to have any more children.

In a scene reminiscent of a slave auction, Celie's stepfather then offers her in marriage to the widower Albert —————, who looks her over like a head of livestock and marries her in desperation because he needs someone to cook and clean for him and take care of his four children. Thus Celie is passed like a piece of property from one cruel and domineering black male into the hands of another. The rest of the novel is Celie's struggle to gain self-respect. At first fighting back does not even seem an option; survival seems the best she can hope for, in this world at least. She stands silent, like a tree, as Mr. ————— beats her, thinking, "That's how come I know trees fear man" (*Purple,* 23). Death seems the only way out of a miserable existence, as Celie tells her daughter-in-law Sofia: "Well, sometime Mr. ————— git on me pretty hard. I have to talk to Old Maker. But he my husband. I shrug my shoulders. This life soon be over, I say. Heaven last always." Sofia's response provides Celie with a rare moment of humor: "You ought to bash Mr. ————— head open, she say. Think bout heaven later." Celie thinks, "Not much funny to me. That funny" (*Purple,* 44).

Celie's ability eventually to stand up to and leave Mr. ————— is due in part to her discovering a definition of God that is large enough to encompass even the poor, ugly black woman that she feels herself to be and in part to her discovering within herself the ability to love and be loved.

Love is noticeably absent from much of Celie's early life. The one person who loves Celie, her younger sister, Nettie, is torn from her when Nettie is first forced from her home by her stepfather's sexual advances and then from Celie's home when she rejects Mr. —————'s. The one gift that Nettie has given Celie, besides her love, is the ability to read and write, Celie having had to quit school the first time she became pregnant. The written word is their one hope of remaining joined to one another, but Mister steals that hope from Celie when, for many years, he hides Nettie's letters. Ignorant of Nettie's whereabouts and unsure that she is even still alive, Celie turns to the only other audience she can think of. Her stepfather has warned her, "You better not tell nobody but God. It'd kill your mammy" (*Purple,* 1). Celie takes him at his word, and the book becomes Celie's growth from her initial passivity to self-affirmation as recorded in her letters to God.

Walker argues, however, that what her critics have failed to see is that Mister, too, changes, that the novel is about the dis-ease that both Celie and Albert —————— suffer from, an illness that derives from the experiences that early shaped their personalities and from their culturally derived sex roles. Walker writes, "They proceed to grow, to change, to become whole, i.e., well, by becoming more like each other, but stopping short of taking on each other's illness" (*Living,* 80). In a 1985 interview in *Ms.,* Walker acknowledges that a feminist director might have made different choices in presenting Celie and her husband, "but Steven [Spielberg], I think, was more interested in showing the transformation of Mister to Albert, as well as Celie's changes . . . I think you really understand Albert better in the movie than in the book" (Dworkin, 95). She admits in "In the Closet of the Soul" that she indeed loves Albert because he "went deeply enough into himself to find the courage to change. To grow" (*Living,* 80). Celie too goes inside herself to find the courage to change and grow.

One of two essays in *Living by the Word* that deal with *The Color Purple* is "Coming in From the Cold," read at both the National Writers Union in New York and the Black Women's Forum in Los Angeles in 1984. Here Walker deals directly with the proposed banning of the novel by the Oakland, California, public schools because a student's mother objected to what she considered to be the book's offensive language. (The book was finally exonerated.) The essay is Walker's defense of her decision to let Celie tell her own story in her own voice—or rather in the voice of Walker's step-grandmother, Rachel, who in her poverty left to Walker as an inheritance only the memory of the sound of her voice.

As Walker explains, to have Celie speak in the language of her oppressors would be to deny her the validity of her existence; to suppress her voice would be to murder her and to attack all those ancestors who spoke as she does. Her words, particularly the opening ones describing her rape by her stepfather, might shock, but they are the only words that she could have used. They are a part of the self that Celie is eventually able to accept. Walker writes of Celie, "She has not accepted an alien description of who she is; neither has she accepted completely an alien tongue to tell us about it. Her being is affirmed by the language in which she is revealed, and like everything about her it is characteristic, hard-won, and authentic" (*Living*, 64). Or as Celie herself tells Albert, "We all have to start somewhere if us want to do better, and our own self is what us have to hand" (*Purple*, 278).

A Twin Self

Primary among the experiences that shape Celie's personality is her mistreatment by men. Out of these experiences grows her disdain for men and, later, for the traditional God modeled in their image.

Early it becomes obvious that she feels little for men except fear. When her stepfather beats her for allegedly winking at a boy in church, she writes, "I don't even look at mens. That's the truth. I look at women, tho, cause I'm not scared of them" (*Purple*, 6). When, after her marriage, another black woman compliments Albert's good looks, Celie writes, "He do look all right, I say. But I don't think about it while I say it. Most times mens look pretty much alike to me" (*Purple*, 16). Sex with Albert holds no pleasure for her, as she tells Shug Avery, Albert's long-time lover:

Mr. —————— can tell you, I don't like it at all. What is it like? He git up on you, heist your nightgown around your waist, plunge in. Most times I pretend I ain't there. He never know the difference. Never ast me how I feel, nothing. Just do his business, get off, go to sleep.

She start to laugh. Do his business, she say. Do his business. Why, Miss Celie. You make it sound like he going to the toilet on you.

That what it feel like, I say. (*Purple*, 81)

Celie's feelings toward men do not initially prevent her accepting without question a God created in the image of man, albeit a white man. At Shug's insistence, she describes what her God looks like: a "big and old and tall and graybearded" white man in long white robes. When Shug laughs, Celie asks, "Why you laugh? . . . What you expect him to look like, Mr. ——————?" (*Purple*, 201). Celie is not able to redefine herself in any but a subservient position until she replaces her fear of men with anger and, in the process, redefines God.

God was the subject of a course, taught by Susan Marie (read Alice Walker), described in "A Letter of the Times, or Should This Sado-Masochism Be Saved?" This short story in letter form from *You Can't Keep a Good Woman Down* is invaluable in explaining how the epistolary form of *The Color Purple* aids Celie's process of self-definition.

In explaining the nature of her course Susan Marie offers this definition of God: "the inner spirit, the inner voice; the human compulsion when deeply distressed to seek healing counsel within ourselves, and the capacity within ourselves both to create this counsel and receive it." In reading several slave narratives, Susan Marie found within them this inner spirit, "this inner capacity for self-comforting, this ability to locate God within" and felt that it demonstrated "something marvelous about human beings" (*GW*, 119). In seeking help from God, Celie is actually seeking counsel within herself.

In "A Letter of the Times," Walker records how Susan Marie came to the idea of God's being innate in all human beings, a belief that Walker shares with her fictional creation.

I suppose this has all been thought before; but it came to me as a revelation after reading how the fifth or sixth black woman, finding herself captured, enslaved, sexually abused, starved, whipped, the mother of children she could not want, lover of children she could not have, crept into the corners of the fields, among the haystacks and the animals, and found within her own heart the only solace and love she was ever to know.

It was as if these women found a twin self who saved them from their abused consciousness and chronic physical loneliness; and that twin self is in all of us, waiting only to be summoned. (*GW*, 119)

Celie is not in a literal sense a slave, but she certainly is "sexually abused, . . . whipped, the mother of children she could not want, lover of children she could not have." In her suffering, as hundreds of slave women before her she finds the twin self within. The letters that constitute the first half of the novel are a one-way correspondence between the abused and lonely Celie and her own inner self—that part of herself that eventually makes her fight back. In writing to God she is writing to the part of her personality growing progressively stronger until she is able to acknowledge the God within herself and demand the respect due her.

First, though, she has to reject her traditional notions of divinity. This she does with the help of Shug Avery.

Switching Roles

In "Writing *The Color Purple*," Walker recalls the exact moment when she came upon the germ of the story that would evolve into her third novel. She and her sister Ruth were hiking through the woods discussing a lovers' triangle that both were aware of when Ruth said, "And you know, one day The Wife asked The Other Woman for a pair of her drawers." Walker knew that suddenly she had the missing piece of the historical novel that had been taking shape in her mind. She anticipated with amusement critics' response to the fact that her "history," in typical womanist fashion, started with one woman's asking another woman for her underwear (*Gardens*, 355–56).

The third point of Walker's central love triangle in *The Color Purple* is the dynamic singer Shug Avery, based in part on Zora Neale Hurston but also in part on Walker's own aunts, who were domestics up north, but who "had wonderful nails, and were all beautifully dressed—just fantastically vibrant women with great perfumes."[2] Walker early knew that she was writing the story of two women who felt married to the same man. What completes the love triangle in all its symmetry is Celie and Shug's love for each other.

Where Celie is not at all attracted to men, she is immediately drawn to Shug, who has been her husband's lover for years. Shug and Albert never married because his lightskinned father disapproved of Shug's dark skin; now her own father considers her a tramp because she has had three children by a man she never married and makes her living singing in juke joints. Celie begins to dream of Shug, though, from the moment she first sees a picture of her. Rather than being pushed farther apart when Albert brings Shug into their home to recuperate from what the town gossips suspect is "some nasty woman disease," Celie and Albert find that their mutual love for Shug draws them closer than ever before.

Celie finds herself aroused by Shug in a way that no man has ever aroused her. Her sexual attraction to Shug is clear the first time she bathes the ailing Shug and feels that she has turned into a man as she gazes at Shug's naked body, feeling that washing her body is a sort of prayer. Looking at Shug's thin black hands, she can hardly resist the temptation to take Shug's fingers into her mouth. She still feels no sexual stirrings for Albert even when they "make love," but the mere thought of Shug is enough to make her feel "something stirring down there" (*Purple*, 69). The only reason she even tries to find some meager joy in sex with Mister is that she knows it is something Shug has shared with him—and liked.

Once Shug succeeds in awakening Celie to her own sexuality, Celie only agonizes more to realize that while she loves Shug, Shug loves

Albert. She tries to convince herself that "that the way it spose to be," but her heart hurts just the same, and she cries as she overhears Shug and Albert making love. Soon, however, she is crying in Shug's arms instead, and talking about love:

> She say, I love you, Miss Celie. And then she haul off and kiss me on the mouth.
> *Um,* she say, like she surprise. I kiss her back, say, *um,* too. Us kiss and kiss till us can't hardly kiss no more. Then us touch each other.
> I don't know nothing bout it, I say to Shug.
> I don't know much, she say.
> Then I feels something real soft and wet on my breast, feel like one of my little lost babies mouth.
> Way after while, I act like a little lost baby too. (*Purple,* 118)

For viewers who have read *The Color Purple,* the movie's opening scene calls to mind the scene from which the novel's title was drawn, another scene that was filmed amidst a field of purple. In this critical scene Shug offers Celie the image of a God human enough to share Celie's need for love and compassionate enough to rejoice with his people when they find it, even in its most blatantly sexual forms:

> God loves all them feelings. That's some of the best stuff God did. And when you know God loves 'em you enjoys 'em a lot more. You can just relax, go with everything that's going, and praise God by liking what you like.
> God don't think it dirty? I ast.
> Naw, she say. God made it. Listen, God love everything you love—and a mess of stuff you don't. But more than anything else, God love admiration.
> You saying God vain? I ast.
> Naw, she say. Not vain, just wanting to share a good thing. I think it pisses God off if you walk by the color purple in a field somewhere and don't notice it.
> What it do when it pissed off? I ast.
> Oh, it make something else. People think pleasing God is all God care about. But any fool living in the world can see it always trying to please us back.
> Yeah? I say.
> Yeah, she say. It always making little surprises and springing them on us when we least expect.
> You mean it want to be loved, just like the bible say.
> Yes, Celie, she say. Everything want to be loved. (*Purple,* 203–204)

Mae Henderson has said of Shug, "Unlike Celie, who derives her sense of self from the dominant white and male theology, Shug is a self-invented character whose sense of self is not male inscribed. Her theology allows a divine, self-authorized sense of self."[3] Celie rejects her own former notion of a white and male God in anger when she learns, with Shug's assistance, that Albert has "stolen" Nettie from her by hiding her letters. Finally reading through the stacks of old letters, Celie learns her real father was lynched and the man she knew as her father was really her stepfather. She is understandably relieved to learn that her children are not her own brother and sister, yet she is angered by all that God has allowed to happen to her. She no longer writes to God and even denies his existence as she explains to Shug why she doesn't.

What God do for me? I ast.
She say, Celie! Like she shock. He give you life, good health, and a good woman that love you to death.
Yeah, I say, and he give me a lynched daddy, a crazy mama, a lowdown dog of a step pa and a sister I probably won't ever see again. Anyhow, I say, the God I been praying and writing to is a man. And act just like all the other mens I know. Trifling, forgitful and lowdown.
She say, Miss Celie, You better hush. God might hear you.
Let 'im hear me, I say. If he ever listened to poor colored women the world would be a different place, I can tell you. (*Purple*, 199–200)

Celie is ready now to accept the genderless God that Shug offers her. Shug points out that she too lost interest in God when she discovered that He was white, and a man. She continues,

Here's the thing, says Shug. The thing I believe. God is inside you and inside everybody else. You come into the world with God. But only them that search for it inside find it. . . .
It? I ast.
Yeah, It. God ain't a he or a she, but a It.
But what do it look like? I ast.
Don't look like nothing, she say. It ain't a picture show. It ain't something you can look at apart from anything else, including yourself. I believe God is everything, say Shug. Everything that is or ever was or ever will be. And when you can feel that, and be happy to feel that, you've found It. (*Purple*, 202–203)

As Wendy Wall points out, this conception of God that both relocates and regenders Him proves that Celie's letters to God, "which have been directed toward the task of creating self," have been appropriately addressed. "Her letters connect her to this interior being."[4] Celie has become the sort of self-invented character Mae Henderson refers to, and her creation of self is one sense in which she will achieve her goal of entering creation when she finally leaves her husband. In another sense she will enter creation by becoming one with all created things, and in her climactic and mystical departure scene she does. She takes on seemingly God-like powers when she curses Mister before going to Memphis with Shug. As she confronts her husband, warning him that all the suffering that he has inflicted on her will be inflicted on him twofold, it is not her voice she hears, but the trees and the wind and the dirt speaking through her. In still another sense, she will enter creation by becoming a creator herself. Tempted at one point to slit Mister's throat for all the evil that he has done, she chooses the needle over the razor and takes advantage of her skill as a seamstress to enter the world of business. As God does when his efforts are taken for granted, she sets out to create something new.

With a sort of neat symmetry possible only in the world of fiction, Nettie meanwhile, half a world away as a missionary in Africa, has also discovered a "more fluid and internal" God, to use Wall's term. Among an African people who worship the roofleaf plant that makes their way of life possible, she has learned that the God that she has tried to introduce them to, the one from the "white folks' bible" that Celie found incompatible with the reality of her life in the rural South, is not necessarily any more compatible with the reality of life in Africa. Near the end of almost 30 years in Africa, Nettie writes to Celie:

God is different to us now, after all these years in Africa. More spirit than ever before, and more internal. Most people think he has to look like something or someone—a roofleaf or Christ—but we don't. And not being tied to what God looks like, frees us.

When we return to America we must have long talks about this, Celie. And perhaps Samuel and I will found a new church in our community that has no idols in it whatsoever, in which each person's spirit is encouraged to seek God directly, his belief that this is possible strengthened by us as a people who also believe. (*Purple,* 264)

Through a miracle of fate and fictional license, Celie's children, Adam and Olivia, are in Africa with their Aunt Nettie because the missionary couple who hired Nettie are the very ones to whom Celie's father sold her children. As the couple explain, "God" sent them the two children. In another convenient trick of fiction, the children's adoptive mother Corinne dies, leaving her husband Samuel free to marry Nettie, thus resolving one of the many secondary love triangles and setting the stage for Celie's whole family to come back to her in one convenient surge. Before that happens, however, Celie has a lot of catching up to do as she reads Nettie's letters from Africa. And there are many, for, as Nettie explains, "[W]hen I don't write to you I feel as bad as I do when I don't pray, locked up in myself and choking on my own heart" (*Purple,* 136).

The epistolary format is difficult to sustain for the whole work, but Nettie serves as a convenient audience to replace the God that Celie has rejected (with the exception of the last letter, which, in its salutation, reflects Celie's newfound pantheism: "Dear God. Dear stars, dear trees, dear sky, dear peoples. Dear Everything. Dear God" [*Purple,* 292]). The remainder of the novel consists of Nettie's accumulated letters and the letters to Nettie that now replace Celie's letters to God. Nettie's letters, in their formal English, seem stiffly didactic after the poetic beauty of Celie's nearly illiterate attempts to verbalize her plight, but they provide a parallel between the oppressive, male-dominated Southern society that Celie has now become strong enough to rebel against and an equally oppressive and male-dominated society in Africa.

Celie's daughter, Olivia, is allowed to go to school in Africa, but education is denied the native Olinka girls. Women are expected to fulfill a subservient role in their village, never looking directly into a man's face. They are defined only in terms of the value they have for their husbands. Nettie is told by one of the Olinka women, "A girl is nothing to herself; only to her husband can she become something." Nettie asks, "What can she become?" and is told, "The mother of his children" (*Purple,* 162). Nettie compares the power the Olinka man has over his wife to the power their stepfather had over her and Celie, and the general desire of the African society to keep women uneducated to the desire of American whites to keep blacks ignorant. The final horror for Nettie and her niece and nephew is the clitoridectomy required of young African women as part of their initiation into adulthood.

According to feminist Mary Daly, some African cultures perform the clitoridectomy in an attempt to remove that which is masculine from the female genitalia (Wall, 87). Wall adds that such genital mutilation is thus an attempt to suggest that gender differentiation is socially inscribed. She continues, "Throughout *The Color Purple,* inherent biological gender characteristics are questioned; gender becomes a socially-imposed categorization" (Wall, 87). This interpretation is in keeping with Walker's claim that both Celie and Albert exist in a state of dis-ease because of socially defined sex roles. They become whole and at peace only when they achieve an androgynous blend of traditionally male and female characteristics. Gender sharing and gender crossover eventually allow Celie and Albert to grow toward wholeness by growing more like each other.

Reversal of gender roles is initially most obvious in the characters Harpo, Albert's son, and Sofia, Harpo's wife. Even as Harpo grows into manhood, Celie, his stepmother, notices that his face begins to look like a woman's face. As soon as Harpo marries the big, strong, and ruddy-looking Sofia, who has already borne him a child, Mister predicts that she will soon switch the traces on him, and she does. Sofia is at home in a man's pants, splitting shingles and working on the roof. (This scene recalls images from Nettie's letter reporting that in the Olinka village the job of thatching roofs belongs to the women.) She prefers field work and even chopping wood to keeping house. (In Africa, Nettie informs Celie, the women are responsible for the crops.) The irony is that Harpo truly enjoys "woman's work," and the two could have been quite content with him cooking and washing dishes and her doing traditional men's work had Mister not raised Harpo to feel less of a man if he was not in control. Harpo cannot simply accept that he and Sofia are happy in their reversed roles—and that love is a far more important element in marriage than obedience—but must rather try to prove his manhood by beating her, as Mister beats Celie, to make her "mind." They fight "like two mens," with Harpo constantly getting the worst of the beating. When he gorges himself with food in an attempt to grow as big as Sofia, he only looks pregnant. "When it due? us ast" (*Purple,* 64).

Sofia finally loses interest in Harpo and, with their five children in tow, leaves him. She eventually goes to jail for striking the white mayor, surviving there only by masking her own natural aggression and pretending instead to be the meek and submissive Miss Celie. When at the end of the novel Harpo and Sofia are together again, they revert to the roles that they are most comfortable with even if society is not, with Sofia clerking in the store that Celie has inherited from her real father and Harpo staying at home.

Celie and Shug, of course, cross traditional gender boundaries as soon as they enter into their lesbian relationship. There is something of the masculine in Shug, in spite of all her flamboyant, feminine charm. She is, for one thing, totally inept at sewing. Shug's mother is raising Shug's three children. Even Celie acknowledges that Shug is manly in her talk at times. On one occasion, Shug greets Sofia with, "Girl, you look like a good time, you do." Celie thinks,

> That when I notice how Shug talk and act sometimes like a man. Men say stuff like that to women, Girl, you look like a good time. Women always talk about hair and health. How many babies living or dead, or got teef. Not bout how some woman they hugging look like a good time.
>
> All the men got they eyes glued to Shug's bosom. I got my eyes glued there too. I feel my nipples harden under my dress. My little button sort of perk up too. Shug, I say to her in my mine, Girl, you looks like a good time, the Good Lord knows you do. (*Purple,* 85)

Shug calls Celie a virgin because she has never found sexual fulfillment even though she has had two children and is married. Thus in Shug's sense of the term, Celie remains a virgin until her sexual union with Shug. As Bernard Bell rightly acknowledges, "rather than heterosexual love, lesbianism is the rite of passage to selfhood, sisterhood, and brotherhood for Celie."[5]

Much later, Albert and Celie discuss their mutual admiration for Shug, but disagree about what constitutes womanliness and manliness:

> Mr. —————— ast me the other day what it is I love so much about Shug. He say he love her style. He say to tell the truth, Shug act more manly than most men. I mean she upright, honest. Speak her mind and the devil take the hindmost, he say. You know Shug will fight, he say. Just like Sofia. She bound to live her life and be herself no matter what.
>
> Mr. —————— think all this is stuff men do. But Harpo not like this, I tell him. You not like this. What Shug got is womanly it seem like to me. Specially since she and Sofia the ones got it.
>
> Sofia and Shug not like men, he say, but they not like women either.
>
> You mean they not like you or me. (*Purple,* 276)

To get Celie's mind off of killing Mister once she learns that he has been hiding Nettie's letters, Shug encourages her to make some pants.

In fact, she encourages her to wear pants because, as she tells Celie, "You don't have a dress do nothing for you. You not made like no dress pattern either." Celie assumes that Mister will not permit his wife to wear pants, but she learns, to her surprise, that Shug used to put on Albert's pants when they were courting—that they were "like a red flag to a bull"—and that, once, he even put on her dress (*Purple*, 152–53). When Celie leaves Albert to move to Memphis with Shug, she soon finds that she can make a living by practicing the traditionally feminine art of sewing, but the pants that she quickly becomes famous for are equally appropriate for men and women. Back home, Mister sinks into such a state of self-pity and drunkenness that Harpo takes over the traditionally feminine duties of cooking and cleaning for him, and even bathing him. At one point Sofia walks in to find Harpo and his father asleep in each other's arms.

Walker has been accused of painting men in a favorable light only when they become too old to be a threat sexually. Celie's heart softens toward Harpo when she hears how he cared for Mister. The extent to which men become likeable is directly proportional, then, not to their age, but rather to the extent to which they take on feminine charac-teristics. The change in the heart of Albert is almost as hard to believe in as the change in the heart of Grange Copeland, but as Celie even-tually has to admit, "If you know your heart [is] sorry . . . that mean it not quite as spoilt as you think" (*Purple*, 289). At the end of the novel Albert is working his fields once again and keeping house for himself, even cooking. He appears late in the novel sewing with Celie on the porch of the house they once shared and actually designing shirts to go with Celie's pants. He recalls that as a child he liked to sew along with his mother until others ridiculed him. Celie tells him that in Africa, after all, men quilt and wear "dresses." She is the one now wearing the pants and smoking a pipe.

Black Is Beautiful

Bernard Bell has pointed out that *The Color Purple* is "more con-cerned with the politics of sex and self than with the politics of class and race. . . . its unrelenting, severe attacks on male hegemony, es-pecially the violent abuse of black women by black men, is offered as a revolutionary leap forward into a new social order based on sexual egalitarianism" (Bell, 263). A part of the self Albert must contend with, however, is undeniably racial, and a part of his acceptance of self is an ability to love that part of himself that his own partially white father most hates.

One of Walker's disappointments with the response to her works has been that many black men proved themselves incapable of empathizing with the black woman's suffering under sexism, but also that, even worse, with *The Color Purple* they seized the opportunity presented by the publicity surrounding the book and the movie to draw attention to themselves as though they were the ones being oppressed. Related to the denial that such sexual brutality exists in the black community is the refusal to accept the fact that blacks are in many cases descended not only from slaves, but also from slave owners. Walker argues that critics too often fail to stop and think about who Albert ———— is; it is even clearer on screen than in print that he is the son of a man who is part white: Old Mr. ————, who inherited and passed down to Albert the run-down plantation house that belonged to his father/master. Walker writes, "Old Mister is so riddled with self-hatred, particularly of his black 'part,' the 'slave' part (totally understandable, given his easily imagined suffering during a childhood among blacks and whites who despised each other), that he spends his life repudiating, denigrating, and attempting to dominate anyone blacker than himself, as is, unfortunately, his son" (*Living,* 81).

If his son is one target of Old Mister's contempt, even more so is Shug Avery, whom he describes as "black as tar." Walker views Albert's love of Shug, in spite of her color and his father's protestations, as a sign of psychic health and, more specifically, a sign of self-love: "Albert's ability to genuinely love Shug, and find her irresistibly beautiful—black as she is—is a major sign of mother love, the possibility of health; and, since she in her blackness reflects him, an indication that he is at least capable of loving himself. No small feat" (*Living,* 81). For Albert as for Celie, learning to love himself is requisite to becoming whole. If Celie's meekness does not make her a saint, neither does Albert's brutality make him a devil. Albert has indeed changed, a point that both Walker and Spielberg want to drive home to their audiences. Even Celie concludes, "He not such a bad looking man, you know, when you come right down to it. And now it do begin to look like he got a lot of feeling hind his face. . . . He ain't Shug, but he begin to be somebody I can talk to" (*Purple,* 280–83). When Albert proposes that they marry again, her response is "Naw, I still don't like frogs, but let's us be friends" (*Purple,* 290).

Celie has never before been at such peace with Albert or with herself. They have shared the sorrow of having lost Shug to someone else. Now Celie knows that she can bear life with or without Shug: "If she come, I be happy. If she don't, I be content. And then I figure this the lesson I was suppose to learn" (*Purple*, 290). Celie is also at peace with God, a point she makes as she explains to an understandably stunned Sofia why she smokes marijuana. "I smoke when I want to talk to God. I smoke when I want to make love. Lately I feel like me and God make love just fine anyhow. Whether I smoke reefer or not.

"Miss Celie! say Sofia. Shock. Girl, I'm bless, I say to Sofia. God knows what I mean" (*Purple*, 227).

Ntozake Shange's closing words in *for colored girls who have considered suicide when the rainbow is enuf* would be fitting ones for Celie at this advanced stage of her psychological development: "i found god in my-self and i loved her fiercely."[6]

Chapter Eight

Remembering Who We Are: *Living by the Word* and *Horses Make a Landscape Look More Beautiful*

The more recent of Walker's two volumes of essays, *Living by the Word* (1988), is a collection of selected writings 1973–1987. An epigraph drawn from African author Ayi Kwei Armah's *Two Thousand Seasons* sets the stage for Walker to expand in the essays on the definition of wholeness that has been at the heart of her previously published works. Where much that Walker has written focuses on the wholeness of the individual, the focus now shifts to include larger wholes as well. The search is no longer simply for the wholeness that gives spiritual health to the individual seeker, although that remains a priority, but also for unity between and among people and peoples and ultimately for unity with the universe itself. (Walker herself, for example, would be happy reincarnated as a blade of grass.)

In the Armah passage, new artists—*fundi*—are being taught the way of the *fundi*. They are told, "Our way . . . is a way that aims at preserving knowledge of who we are, knowledge of the best way we have found to relate each to each, each to all, ourselves to other peoples, all to our surroundings. . . . Our way is reciprocity. The way is wholeness." The essays that follow are Walker's observations on "who we are" as individuals, as races, and as a species, and on what who we are bodes for the future of the planet. She has called the collection the record of her journey in search of the planet she knew and loved as a child. She turns to a rather unlikely spokesman to verbalize her hope for the future of her planet: Daniel Ortega, who wrote, "The victory belongs to love" (*Living,* Epigraph).

The Search for Psychic Wholeness

In "In the Closet of the Soul," Walker writes, "Regardless of who will or will not accept us, including perhaps, our 'established' self, we must be completely (to the extent it is possible) who we are. And who we are becomes more obvious to us, I think, as we grow older and more open to the voices of suffering from our own souls" (*Living,* 82).

Suffering can result from trying to deny a part of what one is, or, as Walker puts it, "To cut anyone out of the psyche is to maim the personality; to suppress any part of the personality is to maim the soul" (*Living,* 85). Part of what Walker has had to come to terms with personally and professionally is the entirety of who she is. She has spent her recent years locating both the Indian and the white within herself.

The Indian has been, predictably, easier to accept. She dedicates her fourth collection of poems, *Horses Make a Landscape Look More Beautiful* (1984), to two people, one of them her part Cherokee great-grandmother, Tallulah.[1]

In the essay "My Big Brother Bill," Walker describes herself as emerging, in 1984, from a long period "of spiritual reassessment and political hibernation," during which "Indians were very much on my consciousness" (*Living,* 42–43). It was a time when she was obsessed with Indian artifacts and folklore and never traveled without an arrowhead on her person.

Walker perceives "Indians [Africans] of Africa" and "Indians of the Americas" as linked in their suffering. In her journal she writes of how she feels linked with Central Americans because of the mixed blood and the personal history of poverty that she shares with them (*Living,* 176–77). Of her Indian friend the late Bill Wahpepah, the "big brother" of the essay's title, she writes, "There was a special affinity between us based on the common intuitive knowledge that, in a sense, all indigenous peoples are, by their attachment to Mother Earth and experience with Wasichus [a Sioux word for "fat takers," or white men], Conquistadors, and Afrikaners, one" (*Living,* 49). According to Walker, "one of the best things happening on the planet" is the effort by the International Indian Treaty Council to open channels of communication among Indians of all continents.

The shared suffering of Indians and blacks becomes apparent in two cases that Walker writes about in *Living by the Word.* One was the 1984 trial of Dennis Banks, at which her friendship with Wahpepah began and which is described in "My Big Brother Bill." Banks, an American Indian movement leader, was being tried for his involvement in a demonstration in Custer, South Dakota, in 1973 that erupted into violence after 150 Indians gathered to protest the verdict in a trial investigating an Indian youth's death caused by a white man. In "Trying to See My Sister," Walker writes of her unsuccessful attempts to visit in prison a black woman, Dessie Woods, who was sentenced in Georgia to 22 years, later reduced to 12, for theft and murder after she shot and killed a white man to prevent him from raping her and her companion.

Walker found, of course, that the black and the Indian cultures shared more than a history of suffering. During her years of hibernation, with their study of Cherokee folklore, Walker was amazed to learn, for example, that the Uncle Remus stories she knew as a child were the same tales found in Cherokee folk literature. Just as the stories united her with her African heritage when she heard her parents relating these tales of the crafty Brer Rabbit, Indian children shared their ancestral heritage in the same way.

One essay in *Living by the Word*, "The Dummy in the Window," is a scathing indictment of Joel Chandler Harris, the white man given credit for creating Uncle Remus and his tales of Brer Rabbit and Brer Fox. Harris lived in Walker's hometown of Eatonton, Georgia, a century before she did. According to Walker's assessment, his crime against her people was that he stole their stories and in doing so stole a part of their heritage and, concomitantly, a part of who they were as a people. One of his offenses against the descendants of slaves was that he put their stories into the mouth of a fictional creation who, as Harris's daughter-in-law describes it, "has nothing but pleasant memories of the discipline of slavery" (*Living*, 28). By presenting their stories through the words of this "invention," Harris committed an even more significant crime against Walker and other blacks who saw the Uncle Remus stories from the segregated balconies of movie theaters when Walt Disney's *Song of the South* brought them to the screen: He made them ashamed of who they were. "And," Walker explains, "this is very serious, because folklore is at the heart of self-expression and therefore at the heart of self-acceptance. It is full of the possibilities of misinterpretation, full of subtleties and danger. And in accepting one's own folklore, one risks learning almost too much about one's self" (*Living*, 32).

In speaking of blacks' need to preserve who they have been in order to understand who they are, Walker pauses to observe that she is probably wrong to attribute this love of memory to any single race or clan. She believes rather that "it is a human trait—and for all I know, even a nonhuman animal one—and that what the black, the Native American, and the poor white share in America is common humanity's love of remembering who we are" (*Living,* 63).

One way to ensure that the memory of ancestors of any race or clan lives on is by preserving their language, their sound. For all those who have suffered under oppression, however, to preserve the language is, of necessity, to reveal the conflict between oppressor and oppressed:

It is because the language of our memories is suppressed that we tend to see our struggle to retain and respect our memories as unique. And of course our language is suppressed because it reveals our cultures, cultures at variance with what the dominant white, well-to-do culture perceives itself to be. To permit our language to be heard, and especially the words and speech of our old ones, is to expose the depth of the conflict between us and our oppressors and the centuries it has not at all silently raged. It is to believe that behind the back of the man who insisted on being called "master," the "slaves" called him "redneck," "devil," and "peckerwood." It is to learn that every time the real Tonto said "How" aloud to the same racist Wasichu, under his breath he added "stupid," "childish," "asinine," or "unintelligent." (*Living,* 63)

Several poems in *Horses Make a Landscape Look More Beautiful* deal with the suffering caused by Wasichus in their various guises worldwide. The Sioux used the term to refer to the white man; in a broader sense it refers to the greedy and destructive of any race. In the poem "Who?" Walker questions whether any group remains untouched by the Wasichu. The hope was that after the Wasichu had invaded people, trees, water, rocks, and air, at least the moon would be safe, but the conqueror has left his footprints even there. Another title from the volume declares, "No One Can Watch the Wasichu," because his destructiveness is both too pervasive and, like the rape of a child, too sickening to watch. In this country, a Wasichu named Chenault killed Mrs. Alberta King, a death commemorated in "Killers" (*Horses,* 26). A world away, Africans cry and bleed in Wasichu mines to produce "The Diamonds on Liz's Bosom."

In "First, They Said," they, the Wasichus, declare a group of villagers savage, immoral, inferior, and backward, yet eventually admit that the very existence of the villagers is an affront. They make the mistake of giving the natives guns in the hope that they will war among themselves and destroy each other. Now the armed natives wait for the next insulting word to come out of a Wasichu mouth.

A jolting experience came for Walker when she heard a Wasichu voice coming from almost within her. As she wrote in trying to explain the character Mister in *The Color Purple,* black people must accept the extent to which they are descendants not only of slaves but of slaveowners as well. What she specifically has had to acknowledge is the white man who was her great-great-grandfather on her father's side. She confronts this white ancestor in the dedication to *Horses* and in another poem in the volume, "Family Of."

Not until Walker was in her 30s did this white ancestor start entreating her for entry into her consciousness, asking whom he had murdered. She in turn "murdered" him successfully, for a time, by refusing to let him in when he came kicking the door and shouting to be admitted. The dedication to *Horses* is her admission that she eventually did let him in, and "In the Closet of the Soul" is her explanation of why.

"In the Closet of the Soul" is, among other things, a response to a 1984 review of *Horses Make a Landscape Look More Beautiful* that K. T. H. Cheatham wrote for the *Richmond News Leader.* Cheatham sees Walker's acknowledgement of her Indian blood as an appeal to the world to be viewed as an Indian rather than as a black and her acknowledgment of the rapist in her bloodline as an example of "the kind of twisted pathology that black psychology is still trying to unravel" (*Living,* 87). She answers the first charge by stating her desire to acknowledge all the varied components of her soul rather than any single one. Just as Celie and Albert in *The Color Purple* existed in a state of disease because of the limitations placed upon them by culturally derived sex roles, individuals who try to deny the mixture of races within themselves often suffer from psychic illness.

In response to the second charge, it is even more important to Walker to acknowledge the rape victim in her background than the rapist; if her great-great-grandmother had to endure rape, she feels the least she can do is mention it. This 11-year-old rape victim is also remembered in the poem "The Thing Itself," where Walker argues that her great-great-grandmother's world had no pornography to teach her that all "real" women like rape—or so the argument goes. In the poem, memories of this child/woman come to mind when Walker's lover playfully threatens to "rape" her and she suddenly comes to see that he, too, in spite of his potential, is a Wasichu.

Walker has had to admit, in both senses of that verb, the white in her. The part of the dedication to *Horses* that Cheatham ignored describes the peace that comes with that admission, with the "peaceful coming together racially, at last, of [her] psyche" (*Living,* 86).

The peace does not exist uninterrupted. Walker writes that at her friend Bill Wahpepah's farewell ceremony, she cried more for herself than for him, envying him the freedom he had found in death: "What a mess the world is in! I thought. What peace to get away!" (*Living,* 48). She believes that when she looked into the faces of the Indians in the Edward S. Curtis photographs that covered the walls of her apartment during her time of spiritual reassessment, their expressions forewarned of the devastation to other human beings and to the environment that was to come. The anger Walker still feels at "the mess the world is in" comes through strongly in both *Living by the Word* and *Horses Make a Landscape Look More Beautiful,* even though each, in the final analysis, looks forward to the future with hope.

A tragic example of the devastation visited by one human being on another was the 1985 bombing of the MOVE (for *Movement,* as in revolutionary movement) house on Osage Avenue in Philadelphia, the "City of Brotherly Love." Hearing of the bombing while she was standing on a street corner in Paris, Walker tried to fathom the depth of a hatred that could have led a black mayor, Wilson Goode, to order the bombing of a house occupied by 13 blacks, including five children. Two occupants survived, including one adult, Ramona Africa, who was badly burned yet who was sentenced to prison for "riot" in spite of the fact that it was her house that was bombed. The title of Walker's essay picks up on a quotation from Ramona Africa: "Nobody Was Supposed to Survive."

Walker admits that, for all her liberalism, living next door to the MOVE members in Philadelphia probably would have been impossible even for her. They were given to profanity and to using bullhorns to harangue the neighbors about the corruption in the American political and social system. They collected stray dogs and believed in letting all organic matter, from watermelon rinds to dead bodies, "cycle" back into the earth naturally, and they didn't believe in diapers for their children. They also wore their hair in dreadlocks and were considered unclean. The media references to their long ropes of hair, their dreadlocks, gave Walker pause, for she too wore dreadlocks in 1985.

Did anything these people did, though, justify the horrible death that they died, caught between the fire inside their house and a barrage of police bullets outside? Walker argues that they died because they tried to live as "a different tribe" (*Living,* 157) within the U. S. political and social system they deplored. They died because they chose a radically different lifestyle. They died ultimately because they represented a part of black America that was an embarrassment even to other black Americans. Walker asks Goode and all others who were shamed by the presence of the MOVE members among them,

> How does it feel to massacre
> the part of yourself
> that is really,
> well—
> considering the nappy hair
>   and watermelon rinds
> and naked black booties
> and all—
> pretty much an embarrassment? (*Living,* 161)

The Whole World in Her Hands

In *Living by the Word,* Walker presents herself, as she presented Meridian, as a woman in the process of changing her mind. After years of longing to be "alone in the middle of fields and forests, silent, without need of words" (*Living,* xix) in an attempt to avoid the daily news of death and despair that seemed the foul breath of the planet itself, Walker has decided not to give up on her planet after all. Her anger has not disappeared—it comes through clearly as she writes about the MOVE slaughter or about the treatment of Dessie Woods—but it is more controlled.

The Walker of *Living by the Word* is ultimately an optimist. In fact, in her preface she thanks "creation" for her optimism. The first poem in *Horses Make a Landscape Look More Beautiful,* "Remember?," sets the optimistic tone for many of the poems in that volume as well when the dark, wounded girl with which it begins evolves into a healed woman who offers two flowers whose roots are Justice and Hope.

Walker the optimist has been there in her fictional worlds all along, so her optimism should come as no surprise. After all, one acknowledged weakness of *The Color Purple* is its too-pat storybook ending. *Meridian,* after all, eventually places her trust in the redeeming power of asexual love. Even Grange Copeland and Albert change for the better. The radical revolutionary of *In Search of Our Mothers' Gardens* who wanted to drop bombs into white laps has mellowed, yes, but the softer, mellower, more romantic Walker was there all the time, wanting happy endings and trusting in the healing power of love.

The anger that remains—and anger does remain—is more focused; the love, on the other hand, is more encompassing. The poem "1971" recalls Walker's days in Mississippi when she and her husband bought a gun to defend themselves and she dreamed of their enemies sprawling bleeding across the floor. Killing to defend oneself seemed natural. Looking back, though, she acknowledges that while killing remains natural, it must also remain difficult lest the "enemy" become an abstraction. She knows now that the "faces" that should have died were the television ones that leered over the mutilated bodies of those they had killed in the name of war. She has learned the lesson that she had Ruth learn in *The Third Life of Grange Copeland,* that selective forgiveness is just as necessary as selective anger.

In the poem "These Days" she worries that she has bad-mouthed white people once too often in her daughter's presence when Rebecca asks her, "Mama, are you a racist?" In talking with a friend named Sheila in the same poem, she cannot deny the anger that still exists within her, but acknowledges it for the destructive force that it is.

The pervading image behind *Living by the Word,* though, is of Walker the latter-day-hippie, in her dreadlocks and yogi pants, throwing open her door and reaching out in an all-encompassing gesture to draw in life in all of its varied human and nonhuman forms. Meridian made the same gesture poetically at the end of her story when she wrote,

> i want to put an end to guilt
> i want to put and [*sic*] end to shame
> whatever you have done my sister
> (my brother)
> know i wish to forgive you. . . . (*Meridian,* 213)

Celie made it at the end of *The Color Purple* when she addressed her last letter, "Dear God. Dear stars, dear trees, dear sky, dear peoples. Dear Everything. Dear God." By the time Walker let her white great-great-grandfather into her consciousness, her Indian great-great-grandmother was already "safely smoking inside [her] heart" (*Living,* 85). Having let both of them in, and thus having put her own "house" in order, she starts reaching out to draw in everyone and everything else in ever-widening circles of unity.

In her attempt, in spite of the remnants of her anger, to reach out to the whole world with her all-encompassing, all-loving, all-forgiving embrace, Walker reaches not only to blacks and Indians, but to two other groups that have been disenfranchised in American society: American Communists and homosexuals.

The film *Seeing Red* is Julia Reichert and Jim Klein's history of the Communist party as revealed through interviews with rank-and-file members and former members. Walker's essay "On *Seeing Red*" was originally written as an introduction to the film at its January 1984 West Coast premiere. It is also a plea that Americans acknowledge those parts of the nation's collective ancestry they would try to deny— their "real ancestors" in contrast to the sanitized stereotypes that distort the truth of who they as Americans are. Some of those real ancestors were the American Communists of the first half of the twentieth century, whom Walker calls "some of our most radical political and *spirited* ancestors" (*Living,* 128). She applauds them as only one of many waves of the movement for justice in America. Americans as a nation, just as the individual of any nationality, will suffer from psychic disease as long as they deny part of who they are. *Seeing Red* teaches them about a part of their collective past they have been encouraged to ignore.

Walker also reaches out to embrace gays and lesbians with understanding and compassion—and delight. She does so most directly in "All the Bearded Irises of Life." Always with a tone of regret does she admit she is unable to relate to other women sexually. She seems to look upon it as a failure on her part that she cannot. While she is well aware of all the shortcomings of men in general, she still, in a rather wearisome way, it seems to her, falls in love with men in particular. She calls Allen her "last man." When they moved to San Francisco, both she and Allen enjoyed the flair that gays gave to Halloween and the blatant and public delight that two men in love could give one another. By the time Walker wrote "All the Bearded Irises of Life" in 1987, however, the bleak reality was that one out of every two gays in San Francisco had AIDS.

Just as she brushes aside barriers based on sex in "All the Bearded Irises of Life," in her poem "Without Commercials" Walker shoves aside the color barrier, admitting that neither white nor black is an inherently bad color, after all. She tells whites to tan themselves in the sun only if it makes them happy to be brown; on the other hand, she tells blacks to bleach their skin only if being brown pleases them. She concludes that each race merely needs to see the other "without commercials."

In the poem "Each One, Pull One," she reaches back into the grave to achieve union with the dead as well as with the living. She speaks out against those who would bury with the mud of oblivion any person "incorrect" enough to be the wrong color or the wrong sex or in love with the wrong person or country. In particular, she speaks out against those who would sully the reputation of the dead or who would sabotage the art of those who write or sculpt or paint the reality of what they see.

In her essay "Coming in from the Cold," Walker cites two passages from reggae singer Bob Marley's song of the same title. He sang, "Don't you let the system make you kill your brotherman," and later, "Why do you look so sad and so forsaken? Don't you know when one door is closed, many more is opened?" In "A Sudden Trip Home in the Spring," Walker presented a beautiful fictional treatment of each individual as the door to his or her familial past. In "Coming in from the Cold" she adds her nonfictional explanation: "But though the system tries to make us kill our brother/sister humans, by distorting their present and obliterating and ridiculing their past, we are, all of us, those doors of which Marley sings" (*Living,* 65–66). American society shut its doors to "the old ones who spoke in ways that today means their exclusion from serious conscious life"—old ones who spoke like Celie or like the Jewish woman with her Yiddish or the Italian-American with his "a" on the ends of words.

The system closed the door on people who sounded like Celie long before I was born. All of us who can *hear* her today open wide the shut doors in ourselves, and in our society.

And when Celie comes through those doors, buffalo soldiers on one side, Shug and Natty Dread and a clutch of dreadlocked Rastas perhaps on the other, and only when Celie comes through those doors; when Celie comes in from the cold of repression, self-hatred, and denial, and only when Celie comes in from the cold—do I come in. And many of you as well. And when all of us and all of the old ones are hugged up inside this enormous warm room of a world we must build very quickly, really, or die of a too shallow mutual self-respect, you will see, with me, through the happy spirits of our grandchildren, such joy as the planet has never seen. (*Living,* 66)

Walker recalls the old spiritual "Will the Circle Be Unbroken," which she listened to as a child. Death breaks the circle of loved ones on earth, the song says, but not in heaven. Loss is inevitable, of course, "but," Walker writes, "I have found that where there is spiritual union with other people, the love one feels for them keeps the circle unbroken and the bond between us and them strong, whether they are dead or alive. Perhaps that is one of the manifestations of heaven on earth" (*Living,* 67). She feels that she has been on better terms with her own father, spiritually, since his death and that her acceptance of him, too, as a part of her has been essential to her own understanding and acceptance of herself.

Walker's 1986 essay "Journey to Nine Miles" records her 1984 visit, with Robert Allen and her daughter Rebecca, to Bob Marley's grave in his native Jamaica. They visited the grave on Christmas Day, "the traditional day of thanksgiving for the birth of someone sacred" (*Living,* 114). Marley was another of the dead with whom Walker felt a stronger bond after his death than when he was living. She writes of Marley, "Here was a man who loved his roots, even after he'd been nearly assassinated in his own country, and knew they extended to the ends of the earth. . . . Here was the radical peasant-class, working-class consciousness that fearlessly denounced the Wasichus (the greedy and destructive) and did it with such grace you could dance to it." She writes of the time after his death that she discovered his music, "I danced with his spirit—so much more alive still than many people walking around. I felt my own dreadlocks begin to grow" (*Living,* 116).

Sometimes, Walker claims in "A Name Is Sometimes an Ancestor Saying Hi, I'm with You," the dead even come back to serve the living as "spiritual helpers." One of Walker's own helpers is Sojourner Truth, the powerful nineteenth-century abolitionist who had escaped from slavery. The two are linked by their concern for women's rights and by their mysticism, but also by their names. Walker points out that *Sojourner* parallels *Walker* in the sense of traveler, journeyer, or wanderer, and that *Alice* means "truth" in Old Greek. These "synchronicities" delighted Walker and gave her a sense of power that came from the name the two share. She adds, "And when I walk into a room of strangers who are hostile to the words of women, I do so with her/our cloak of authority—as black women and beloved expressions of the Universe (i.e., children of God)—warm about me. . . . This feeling of being loved and supported by the Universe in general and by certain recognizable spirits in particular is bliss. No other state is remotely like it. And perhaps that is what Jesus tried so hard to teach: that the transformation required of us is not simply to be 'like' Christ, but to *be* Christ" (*Living,* 98).

Dear Everything, Dear God

Having tried to break down some of the barriers that people put up between one another, Walker goes a step further in her attempt to merge with the universe by trying to break down what she considers to be the rather artificial barrier between human and nonhuman. If the writer's pen is the microphone held up to the mouths of ancestors (*Living,* 170), it can also be a means of recording the lives of stones and animals and plants, all of whom, according to Walker, can communicate with humans quite well, given the chance.

That animals can communicate with people is a fact children raised around animals know instinctively but adults tend to forget. In fact, Walker looks upon animals as completed creations, as least compared to flawed humanity. The title of *Horses* is a quote from Lame Deer, who explains that having no word for the horse that the white man brought, the Indians called it "holy dog" and could almost forgive the white man for bringing the Indians whiskey because he also brought the horse in all its natural beauty.

The first essay in *Living by the Word,* "Am I Blue?," records the anguish that the white horse that lived in the pasture next to Walker's property near San Francisco felt when his mate was taken away from him and the resulting hatred in his eyes that alone could make him truly look like a beast. On the other hand, Walker is firmly convinced that the two horses on the ranch across the road responded with joyful recognition whenever she passed by after she read "Am I Blue?" in public, thereby revealing her sympathy for her nonhuman friends. In Walker's vision of a perfect universe, freedom and justice would extend to nonhuman animals as well as to human ones. During recent years Walker has attempted, largely with success, to become a vegetarian. "Not Only Will Your Teachers Appear, They Will Cook New Foods for You" and "Why Did the Balinese Chicken Cross the Road?" are two of her works in defense of vegetarianism.

And then there are the trees, major presences in several works in both *Living by the Word* and *Horses.* In the poem "Listen," the speaker's lover, in another life, would choose to come back only as a rock or a tree, yet for her, this student of life, he already is. In the poem "Torture," she advises her readers to plant a tree each time a mother, father, brother, or sister is tortured and, when the trees themselves are tortured, to start a new forest.

To Walker's way of thinking humankind has already started to torture the trees. When she lived in the northern hills of California, she daily saw loggers' trucks, which she describes as hearses, carrying "the battered bodies of the old sisters and brothers" (*Living,* 141). On the other hand, she immediately felt at peace in China when she noted the lines of trees five and six rows deep "for one feels irresistibly drawn to people who would plant and care for so many millions of trees. . . . Because, for one thing, the planting of trees demonstrates a clear intention to have a future and a definite disinterest in war" (*Living,* 101).

Walker the environmentalist is at her best—or her worst, depending on one's perspective—in "Everything Is a Human Being," a dialogue between Walker and the gnarled, diseased old trees she gazes at as she lies across the path in a national park while other tourists detour around her. What the trees tell her is that when it comes to human beings, trees do not discriminate; all people must share the guilt for the destruction being done to the planet and all its life forms. Walker fought against her blood ties to the Wasichus in part because she perceived them as killers and destroyers of the planet. Here she attacks the Wasichus once again, this time for their rape of the land, in contrast to the Native Americans, who viewed everything on earth, even snakes, as their relatives and lived in a respectful relationship with the land for centuries before the white man intruded. The modern Wasichus, Walker argues, still let their greed for profit lead to the destruction of our nation's forests and wildlife and to atrocities such as off-shore drilling, toxic waste dumping, and nuclear arms production.

"Everything Is a Human Being" is a plea for freedom and justice for the entire Earth:

Our thoughts must be on how to restore to the Earth its dignity as a living being; how to stop raping and plundering it as a matter of course. We must begin to develop the consciousness that everything has equal rights because existence itself is equal. In other words, we are all here: trees, people, snakes, alike. . . . The Wasichu's uniqueness is not his ability to "think" and "invent"—from the evidence, almost everything does this in some fashion or other—it is his profound unnaturalness. His lack of harmony with other peoples and places, and with the very environment to which he owes his life. (*Living,* 148–49)

Walker yearns for a time when people had the luxury and dignity of dying naturally, of old age. If Earth's inhabitants today improved the quality of the environment to the point where they could die of old age, the process would automatically preserve the planet's health.

The closing poem in *Horses*—and one of the most successful poems in the volume—is "These Days," or "Some words for people I think of as friends." Those friends include, of course, Robert Allen and Rebecca, but also Belvie Rooks, one of Walker's partners in Wild Trees Press; Gloria Steinem of National Organization for Women (NOW) fame and Walker's friend from her *Ms.* magazine days; her friend, Jan, the potter; Susan Kirschner, another friend and traveling companion; and John, Yoko, and Sean Lennon. The roll call crosses boundaries of race, religion, and sex. Her point: that these are the people whom the world must be saved for. Concern for the planet makes comrades of individuals who in another time and place might have been separated by a range of socially imposed barriers.

Unfortunately Walker, the would-be savior of the planet, at times looks rather foolish and eccentric as she munches seaweed straight off the rocks on the beaches of California or lies across a path in a national park talking to the trees or considers changing her name to Treeflower or Weed. In "Oppressed Hair Puts a Ceiling on the Brain" she discourses on hair as an obstacle to unity with the universe. She mars a lovely piece about her fear that her daughter's smoking will kill her just as it killed Walker's own father by digressing to express sympathy for the poor tobacco plant, enslaved on plantations just as Walker's human ancestors were. Ultimately it may be easier to relate to the angry young Walker of the 1960s than to the aging flower child of the 1980s.

Still, a sincerity is found in her devotion to the environmental cause and to the cause of peace that led to her arrest in 1987 for joining others—most of them white, she notes—blocking one of the gates of the Concord Naval Weapons Station in California. She feels a genuine anguish over what is being done to the planet in the name of progress. Yet a sense of peace pervades—a peace born in part of the reconciliation of her soul with the totality of who she is racially but also a peace that comes from her sense of oneness with the universe.

In a 31 August 1984 journal entry she speaks directly to some creative force in the universe that she stops short of calling God but that
blesses her and her own creative effort. The whole of the story "The
Hair Artist" has just come to her in her meditations, and she responds
with both humility and pride—a pride that she defines as the feeling
of being "overjoyed, thrilled at this gift that seems to say I still know
you. And you know me, in the sense of letting me feel creation along
with you. . . . There is no doubt in my mind that I am blessed. That
you are present in the cosmos and in me and that we are breathing
together—conspiracy. I see now what is meant by faith and the giving
up on the self to the spirit. I thank you for your gifts" (*Living*, 52–
53).

At times she fools herself into thinking that she can stop writing.
In a January 1984 journal entry she addresses the same "great spirit":
"Next month I will be forty. In some ways, I feel my early life's work
is done, and done completely. The books that I have produced already
carry forward the thoughts that I feel the ancestors were trying to help
me pass on. . . . Great spirit, I thank you for the length of my days
and the fullness of my work. If you wanted me to move on, come
home, or whatever is next, I would try to do it joyfully" (*Living*, 95).

In the poem "I Said to Poetry," she tries to say "no" to the creative
muse when it comes and even threatens to turn to prayer instead. Poetry personified gets the upper hand by pointing out that poetry and
prayer are one and the same. Walker has indeed come to see her work
as prayer. She still believes, as she did when she wrote *Once,* that poetry
saves lives. Poems also exist, she explains in "How Poems Are Made/
A Discredited View," as a repository for leftover love.

Living by the Word is in part a record of Walker's travels to see more
of the world she loved. The essay "A Thousand Words" is a series of
verbal snapshots of China in 1983, each, in theory at least, the thousand words that a picture is worth. One of the major ironies of the
collection is that she and her traveling companion Susan Kirschner felt
most at peace sitting in the middle of T'ien An Men Square in Beijing.
Walker's optimism about the future of the planet must have been sorely
tested when the peace of T'ien An Men Square was shattered by the
horrifying events of 4 June 1989.

Chapter Nine

Harmony of Heart and Hearth:
The Temple of My Familiar

Temple of My Familiar (1989) is likely to remain a novel often begun and seldom finished. Any novel that attempts to provide a spiritual history of the universe hardly makes for light reading. One that also demands a belief in transmigration of souls is doubly difficult. Place all that within the context of what Walker herself has called "a romance of the last 500,000 years," and the extent of the challenge the novel presents to its readers begins to emerge.

In *Temple,* Walker brings back from *The Color Purple* some characters whom she simply could not bear to abandon, most notably Miss Celie and Miss Shug. Yet, in spite of the familiar faces that may bring pleasant glints of recognition to *The Color Purple* admirers, the coincidences of fate that bring them into contact with Walker's new characters call for a willing suspension of disbelief that may be too much to ask.

Still, close readers of Walker's works should not have been surprised by the turn that her work took with *Temple of My Familiar.* In fact, *Temple* provides not so much a turn as a logical extension of what had gone before. Once Walker had shown her female characters capable of breaking the bonds of oppression and defining themselves as whole persons, and once she had, at the same time, discovered divinity in all human and nonhuman elements of the universe, it was actually a small step to making women into goddesses. With one possible exception, the novel's goddesses constitute part of womankind's distant past, yet the ancient matriarchal religions discovered by Walker's contemporary characters in the novel allow them to redefine relationships between the sexes. They are thus able to cure themselves of some of the same varieties of dis-ease based on societal expectations that plagued characters in Walker's earlier works. The lessons they learn about the need for balance between the flesh and the spirit help them redefine themselves.

As Walker's own description of the novel indicates, *Temple of My Familiar* is essentially a story of the lives and loves of three couples:

the popular musician Arveyda, with his exotic blend of African/Scots/
Blackfoot/Mexican/Filipino/Chinese blood, and his South American
wife, Carlotta; Suwelo, Carlotta's lover and a history professor, and his
wife, Fanny, Miss Celie's granddaughter and an academic who leaves
teaching literature to become a masseuse; and the elderly black couple,
Miss Lissie and Mr. Hal, friends of Suwelo's Uncle Rafe, whose death
draws Suwelo into their lives. By means of her conversations and correspondence with Suwelo, Miss Lissie serves as Walker's most direct
link to romance and all of life's other complexities as they have existed
over the last half million years.

The Pattern of Freedom

Walker records in her journal that in February 1987 she had been
reading Shirley MacLaine's *Dancing in the Light.* This book may have
had little or nothing to do with the fact that in the Walker novel that
appeared two years later one of the main characters, Miss Lissie, shares
with MacLaine the memory of numerous past lives (*Living,* 132).
Where Walker sees MacLaine's spirituality as limited by her racism—
MacLaine was, for example, frustrated in one of her incarnations by
Africans who were not as advanced as she was—Miss Lissie suffers from
her own brand of racism: She boasts of the fact that in every one of
her incarnations she has been fortunate enough to have been a black
woman.

Miss Lissie's memory of past lives provides a convenient if artificial
means of encapsulating in a single character centuries of the history of
black womanhood. Here is a soul that in one incarnation survived the
horrors of the slave ship only to die on a Virginia plantation after losing
a leg to a bear trap while trying to escape. In another she was a Mooress
burned at the stake as a witch during the Spanish Inquisition. In still
another she was fortunate enough to marry a man of her own choosing,
but because she was born without a hymen and there were no blood-
stained sheets to show the villagers after the marriage was consum-
mated, she was denounced publicly, forced into prostitution, and died
of infection and exposure at age 18.

Looking back over her collective past, Miss Lissie realizes she can
recall few times when she was at peace. One such time was when she
was pygmy in Africa's ancient past. As a pygmy, she viewed the apes
in the jungle as her "cousins." In fact, in her account, the peace-loving
and gentle apes are superior to their rather loud and contentious human

counterparts. While men and women were segregated in the human community, family unity was an important element of simian life. Miss Lissie recalls breaking with her tribe and taking up permanent residence among the apes because she and her mate chose to live together and, as a couple, raise their children, a sort of cohabitation unheard of among humans during that era, but one that gradually came into vogue for a time, as Miss Lissie explains to Suwelo:

It was this way of living that gradually took hold in all the groups of people living in the forest, at least for a very long time, until the idea of ownership—which grew out of the way the forest now began to be viewed as something cut into pieces that belonged to this tribe or that—came into human arrangements. Then it was that men, because they were stronger, at least during those periods when women were weak from childbearing, began to think of owning women and children. This very thing had happened before, and our own parents had forgotten it, but their system of separating men and women was a consequence of an earlier period when women and men had tried to live together—and it is interesting to see today that mothers and fathers are returning to the old way of only visiting each other and not wanting to live together. This is the pattern of freedom until man no longer wishes to dominate women and children or always have to prove his control. (*Temple*, 87–88)

Walker's history of the world as traced through both the novel's African and South American characters records this "pattern of freedom," an alternating between times when men and women could and did live together more or less in harmony and times when harmony was best maintained by living apart. Man's need to dominate (read, dethrone) woman recurs periodically, however, and each time the two sexes enter a period of uneasy cohabitation.

In her story of the middle passage, Miss Lissie recalls a time before Islam became the accepted religion of Africa when the mother was an object of worship. In fact, among the slaves in the ship's hold were those who had been sold into slavery because of their belief in the ancient religion of motherworship. Whole families who worshiped the Goddess of Africa "were routinely killed, sold into slavery, or converted to Islam at the point of the sword" (*Temple*, 195). Lissie tells Suwelo of the subsequent death, during the hundreds of years of the slave trade in Africa, of motherworship: "There were, in the earliest days, raids on the women's temples, which existed in sacred groves of trees, with the women and children dragged out by the hair and forced to marry into male-dominated tribes. The ones who were not forced to do this were either executed or sold into a tribe whose language was different. The men had decided that they would be creator, and they went about dethroning women systematically" (*Temple,* 63–64).

According to Miss Lissie, following the persecution of motherworshipers in Africa, the Moors in Spain mistakenly believed that Spanish Christians "would let the Goddess of Africa 'pass' into the modern world as 'the Black Madonna.' After all, this was how the gods and goddesses moved from era to era before. . . . Some of [our African fathers] pushed on into France and Germany, Poland, England, Ireland, Russia. . . . If I am not mistaken it is only in Poland that Our Black Lady, the Great Mother of All—Mother Africa, if you will—is still openly worshiped. Perhaps that is why it is said of the Poles that they are none too bright" (*Temple,* 195–96).

Except for the Poles, Europeans were apparently not prepared to accept a black mother for their white Christ and thus burned at the stake the daughters of the Moors, claiming that both their color and their gender allied them with the devil. Recalling their African Eden, the women sought solace by talking to the animals with whom they had once felt a kinship, yet that sense of kinship with the nonhuman only added to their persecution. Consorting with animals became a crime punishable by burning at the stake. Yet, "there was something about the relationship she had with animals and with her children that deeply satisfied woman. It was of this that man was jealous" (*Temple,* 198–99).

Although many of Miss Lissie's lives remain quite vivid in her memory, some were lived in times so long past that she calls them *dream memories.* Near the time of her death she confides to Suwelo that in one of these dream memories she was not a woman, but a lion, a woman's familiar. Thus she witnessed firsthand how man's jealousy and his need for dominion changed once again the pattern of freedom. The animals that had shared the warmth of a nightly fire with the women and their children were driven from that circle of warmth, and all were the poorer for the loss:

We grew up together and frequently shared our favorite spots in the forest, or stared by night into the same fire. But this way of life was rapidly ending, for somehow or other by the time I was fully grown, and big, as lions tend to be, the men's camp and the women's had merged. And they had both lost their freedom to each other. The men now took it on themselves to say what should and should not be done by all, which meant they lost the freedom of their long, undisturbed, contemplative days in the men's camp; and the women, in compliance with the men's bossiness, but more because they now became emotionally dependent on the individual man by whom man's law now decreed they must have all their children, lost their wildness, that quality of homey ease on the earth that they shared with the rest of the animals.

In the merger, the men asserted themselves, alone, as the familiars of women. (*Temple,* 364–65)

Miss Lissie mourns the loss of the friendship that she, as a lion, had with women, pitying the poor women left alone with no fellow creatures but men. Still, she admits that she was relieved to escape the "eternity of strife" that men and women, merged, had inaugurated: "In consorting with man, as he had become, woman was bound to lose her dignity, her integrity. It was a tragedy. But it was a fate lions were not prepared to share" (*Temple,* 366).

Miss Lissie has kept this part of her past a secret from her husband, Hal, because he has an irrational but debilitating fear of cats. Her many past lives were once captured on film by a photographer with whom Miss Lissie had an affair and a child. The photographer was mystified by the fact that Miss Lissie appeared to be a different woman in every picture that he took, even to her height and skin color. Occasionally Miss Lissie had to destroy a photograph that came too close to that part of the truth that she was trying to hide from Hal.

In contrast, Miss Lissie never had to hide any part of her self or her selves from Suwelo's Uncle Rafe. She says, "He loved the total me. None of my selves was hidden from him, and he feared none of them." She concludes, "So, loving Rafe and being loved by Rafe was the experience of many a lifetime. And very different from being loved by Hal, even when our passion for each other was at its height, Hal loved me like a sister/mystic/warrior/woman/mother. Which was nice. But that was only part of who I was. Rafe, on the other hand, knowing me to contain everybody and everything, loved me wholeheartedly, as a goddess. Which I was" (*Temple,* 370–71).

Rafe precedes Hal in death, and at her death Miss Lissie leaves for Hal a clue to her hidden feline past in the form of five pictures of lions that she has painted. It remains for Suwelo to fill Hal in on the entirety of the woman who was Miss Lissie. Hal weeps to learn that Miss Lissie never felt that she could be her whole self with him. He is almost blind

by that time; when Suwelo hands him one of the five paintings, he
holds it upside down and can see only a single reddish spot.

Suwelo takes up the painting, which he loves, turns it right side up, and
looks straight into Miss Lissie's dare-to-be-everything lion eyes. He knows,
and she knows, that Mr. Hal will be able to see all of her someday, and so she
and Suwelo must simply wait, and in the meantime . . . she and he can while
away the time contemplating the "reddish spot," which marks the return of
Mr. Hal's lost vision. For on Lissie's left back paw, nearly obscured by her
tawny, luxuriant tail, is a very gay, elegant, and shiny red high-heeled slipper.
(*Temple*, 416)

The marriage between Miss Lissie and Hal, in all of its unorthodoxy,
is presented as the closest to a fulfilling marriage that exists in the
novel. What sustains their love is Hal's unwillingness to destroy in
Miss Lissie the wildness of the lioness that he never knew, his understanding that she can never be emotionally dependent on any one man.
As he watches the suffering she endures bearing their daughter, Lulu,
he knows that never again will he cause her such pain. He is there to
deliver each of her other children, but he does not father them. After
Lulu's birth he never again makes love to Miss Lissie. Theirs is a union
of spirit, however, so complete that bodily union becomes insignifi-
cant. When each gives Suwelo a self-portrait, the artists' signatures
reveal that Hal has painted Miss Lissie's self-portrait and she his. Such
is the closeness of their souls. The portraits themselves are unique, for
while one shows the outline of a woman and the other the outline of a
man, the outlines surround empty blue space.

Harmony of Hearth

Walker explained to Gregory Jaynes in a 1989 interview that the
last scene in *Temple of My Familiar*, where Suwelo and Hal share the
painting of Miss Lissie as a lion, came to her one day while she was
taking out the trash. What came to her in a flash was that older men
have failed in their responsibility to younger ones by not teaching them
how to live. She thought of the old men, "the gentle old men, the
ones who have really grown wise and beautiful"—like her grandfathers—who nevertheless discard or lose their wisdom without passing
it on (Jaynes, 64). Suwelo, this history professor who has never read a
book by a woman and doesn't care to, like the male characters in

"Porn" and in "Coming Apart," has a very long way to go in his thinking about women. It is ultimately to his credit that his soul is not so
"spoilt" that he cannot learn the lessons his elders have to teach. His
lessons come from Hal, but even more so from Miss Lissie.

When Suwelo, a member of the history faculty at a California university, first sees Carlotta, a member of the women's studies depart-
ment, he thinks of her as a Latina Coretta King. Later he realizes that
he was attracted to her because she was a woman of color, yes, "but
one without the kind of painful past that would threaten his sense of
himself as a man or inhibit his enjoyment of her as simply a woman"
(*Temple*, 130). In perceiving her as a woman without a painful past, he
could not have been further from the truth, for in her own immediate
and personal past she has just endured the humiliation of learning that
her husband, Arveyda, is in love with her mother, Zede. And her
South American culture, as revealed by Zede to Arveyda, shares with
Miss Lissie's its matriarchal roots but also its history of pain produced
by man's jealousy of woman and his resulting need to dethrone her.

Zede tells Arveyda of a time in the history of her South American
country when women were priestesses of a *mujer muy grande,* a goddess
who produced the earth. The birth process was a mystery to men, even
though it sometimes produced little beings more like them than like
the women. Ironically, it was the men who made women into priestesses because "what the mind doesn't understand, it worships or fears."
Only a creature proven capable of giving birth, to their way of thinking, could have given birth to the earth. "And so, if the producer of
the earth was a large woman, a goddess, then women must be her
priests, and must possess great and supernatural powers" (*Temple*, 49).

Over time, the men forgot that they were the ones who had elevated
women to the status of goddesses and priests. Living apart from the
women, visiting them only to be played with sexually, taking in each
resulting man-child as soon as it was old enough to leave its mother,
spoiling the fashion-conscious women by providing the feathers,
bones, bark, and animal teeth and claws with which they adorned
themselves, the men soon tired of the women they worshiped. Spying
on the women, they learned the secret of birth and started mutilating
their own bodies in an attempt to redesign them in the image of woman's body. Thousands died in an effort to carve into their bodies the
passage through which new life emerged.

By the time of Carlotta's grandmother, Zede the Elder, men and
women had reversed roles, and men had become priests of a joyless and

spiritless religion. The only remnant of man's worship of the mother was the vague memory that priests must be somehow feminine: "What they remembered was that they must be like women, and if they castrated themselves at a certain age—the time of puberty, when they chose or were chosen for the priesthood—they could sound like woman and speak to the universe in woman's voice" (*Temple,* 51).

Where the men once hunted in order to bring women the means of ornamenting themselves, women such as Zede the Elder now use their creative talents to adorn the male priests. The only truly bright moments of village life come when the priests parade in their feathered, beaded, and shell-bedecked costumes.

Zede the Elder's relationship to her family is reminiscent of the time when women and men lived apart. When she is creating the priests' capes and headdresses out of feathers—"doing holy work"—she draws apart into a separate mud hut for days at a time, lapsing out of her creative state periodically to return to the main house to become a wife and mother for a time. When a new creative phase begins, she sits for days staring into the surrounding banana fields and smoking her clay pipe. "Then eventually she would knock out her pipe—she had a set of chimes, very low, very sweet—and she would knock the pipe against these chimes, which hung beside the door, and she would listen to the sweet, light sound, and then, if she agreed with the sound, she would nod, once, and then she would begin" (*Temple,* 47).

Zede the Younger escapes a revolution in her country and a prison camp where she is sent for a time and where Carlotta is conceived and makes her way to San Francisco. There Zede works days in a sweatshop but at night practices the art passed down to her by her mother. Carlotta first catches a glimpse of one of her mother's magnificent feathered headdresses when the gays parade on Halloween in a scene reminiscent of the parade of effeminate South American priests. Carlotta meets Arveyda during her last year in college when she delivers a cape of peacock feathers her mother has created for him (gays and rock stars, not priests, are her primary clientele). Arveyda has a matching cape made for Carlotta, and in their finery they too parade on Halloween through the streets of San Francisco. Before long they are married and have two children.

After Arveyda drops Carlotta for her mother, Carlotta puts on another type of costume. Later she admits that for a time she was a "female impersonator," putting on the outward garb that would make her attractive to men. She tells Arveyda, "I wore the kind of shoes you'd asked me to wear, though they hurt and you'd left me for my mother, who always wore flats. . . . It didn't make any sense, wearing the shoes. They were killers. But even if they destroyed my feet and crippled my legs, I knew I wasn't giving them up. I liked the way men looked at me in high heels. The look in their eyes made me forget how lonely I was. How discarded." Fanny tells her that she wore the heels as an act of penance, that "women wear things that hurt them to atone for the sin of loving someone they'd rather not" (*Temple*, 294).

The ultrafeminine facade merely makes it easier for Suwelo to use Fanny. He recalls,

She was so superfeminine, in the old style, that it was as if she'd never noticed there was any other way a woman could be. She wore these three-inch heels every day. I'm talking serious stiletto. She even cooked—and I saw this after she let me go home with her—in three-inch heels. Three-inch heels are designed to make a man feel like all he needs to do is push gently and a woman is on her ass. . . . She wore sweaters that followed every curve of her luscious body. Sweaters that dipped. Skirts that clung. Short skirts. Makeup. Earrings. False eyelashes sometimes. (*Temple*, 244)

Suwelo finds it easy to link Carlotta in his mind with the pornography he delves into while his wife is away on an extended trip to Africa: "I'd seen women like her, lissome, tan, with tiny flat waists and high breasts, in magazines and naked onstage. In a way, whenever I looked at her, I saw those other women" (*Temple*, 246).

While Suwelo realizes that he is using Carlotta, she is equally convinced that she is using him. She later tells Fanny that when Fanny returned from Africa and he went back to her, she could have murdered Suwelo, but that "all along he was just a figment of my imagination. A distraction from my misery. He was just 'something' to hold on to; to be seen with; to wrestle with on the kitchen floor." Fanny, the third member of Walker's typical love triangle, sees the irony in what Carlotta reveals: "She thinks how Suwelo believes she took advantage of Carlotta and how this is what she herself had thought. They were both wrong. There had not been a victim and an oppressor; there'd really been two victims, both of them carting around lonely, needy bodies that were essentially blind flesh" (*Temple*, 386).

Suwelo and Carlotta's relationship is as lacking in genuine spirit as Hal and Miss Lissie's is filled with it. Where Carlotta describes Suwelo as a mere figment of her imagination, Suwelo declares her a being of no substance. Miss Lissie, however, makes him realize that he must ask Carlotta's forgiveness, for "it is a sin to behave as if a person whose body you use is a being without substance. 'Sin' being denial of another's reality of who and what she or he actually is" (*Temple,* 353). Lissie traces much of Suwelo's own pain to the fact that he is a fragmented being, in spite of the fact that his name is the same as the rune for *wholeness.* Like other Walker characters, and like Walker herself, Suwelo has tried to close doors to his past, close them against memory and pain. In his case, his parents wait behind that closed door. Miss Lissie tells him that it is the memory of his mother's "abandoned and suffering face" that has made him fear knowing too much of women's pain.

When Suwelo does go in search of Carlotta, he finds that the female impersonator is most definitely gone. Her hair is now that of a concentration-camp survivor. Gone are her sexy clothes and even her voluptuous curves, "her slender, flat-breasted body [now] as vulnerable as a flower." Suwelo tells her that she doesn't even look like a woman anymore. "Obviously," she retorts, "this is how a woman looks" (*Temple,* 398).

Here at the end of the novel Suwelo and Carlotta join with an intimacy they never experienced when they approached each other merely as blind flesh. Theirs is now an intimacy of the spirit, and Suwelo even undergoes a symbolic spiritual rebirth when he plunges into the hot tub they have been sharing and holds himself beneath the warm water for several moments. As Carlotta, her disguises gone, discusses her mother Zede, he feels the door that has barred his own mother from his memory opening a crack. When he is able to talk to Carlotta about his parents, his mother finally walks through that door. Suddenly he recalls the incident he has shut out of his memory, the incident that has made him long to use women's bodies without having to confront the reality of women's pain. He remembers looking down at the bodies of his parents as they lay in the funeral home after being killed in a car wreck, or, as Suwelo calls it, a people wreck. Suwelo recalls being in the car time after time with his drunken father speeding down the road and his mother begging him to let her and her son out. He recalls hating his mother for not trying to get out of their miserable marriage, but as he looks at her lifeless hands with their bloodied and broken nails he realizes that this last time she at least tried to get out of the car and that his father crashed the car into a tree while trying to stop her.

The image of his father that has always loomed large in Suwelo's memory is of a man who had been a World War II soldier and had returned having lost "half of one arm and all of his mind." The one who now looms in the doorway trying to get in is a younger man, one who is not old or drunk, but a handsome young man with two arms. He tells his son, "My name was once Suwelo, too" (*Temple,* 402–403). Seeing his father young and whole once again allows Suwelo to collect some of the fragments of his own reality and let the door to his past swing open.

Miss Lissie, with the wisdom of the ages, had seen the need in Suwelo to open the door to his past. She had also seen that his denial of the past prevented his becoming more than blind flesh. She had written, "For really, Suwelo, if our parents are not present in us, consciously present, there is much, very much about ourselves that we can never know. It is as if our very flesh is blind and dumb and cannot truly feel itself. Intuition is given little validation; instinct is feared. We do not know what to trust, seeing none of ourselves in action beyond our own bodies" (*Temple,* 353). What Miss Lissie did not foresee was that he would open his heart and soul not to Fanny, but to Carlotta. What Carlotta did not foresee was what would become of her mother. Where Suwelo reveals to her his family's past, she reveals to him her family's present: Zede the Younger, Carlotta's mother, has married a shaman in Mexico; Zede the Elder has become one.

Carlotta has rediscovered her creative roots. When she heard the story of her grandmother's pipe and chimes, she decided to become a bell chime player. In Arveyda's studio she shows Suwelo her instruments, wind chimes of all shapes, sizes, colors, and descriptions from all over the world, which she plays with a hardwood stick. She lives in Arveyda's guest house, down a path and across a ravine from the main house, and she is as happy as she has ever been.

At the end of the novel, Carlotta and Arveyda are still married, yet maintaining separate residences. Fanny and Suwelo, their close friends by now, are divorced, yet living together an hour's drive away. They are building a house modeled on the prehistoric ceremonial house of the Ababa tribe, "a house designed by the ancient matriarchal mind and the first heterosexual household ever created. It has two wings, each complete with its own bedroom, bath, study, and kitchen; and in the center there is a 'body'—the 'ceremonial' or common space. . . . After thousands and thousands of years of women and men living apart, the Ababa had, with great trepidation, experimented with the two tribes living, a couple to a household, together. Each person must remain free, they said. That is the main thing. And so they had designed a dwelling shaped like a bird" (*Temple*, 395).

Harmony of Heart

Where Suwelo's affair with Carlotta is flawed by their tendency to view one another as blind flesh, his relationship with his wife, Fanny, is disrupted by her disturbing habit of falling in love with spirits. Her spirit lover of the moment may be an Indian chief dead for a century or a spirit that doesn't even know who or what it is. When Suwelo tries to explain his problem to an impassive Jewish psychiatrist, he stops short of adding that Fanny's lovers don't even have to be people; "he thought he'd save Fanny's attachment to trees and whales until he could see further" (*Temple*, 184).

Like Suwelo, Fanny needs to open locked doors inside of herself. Where Suwelo's parents wait behind the closed door of his soul, from behind Fanny's closed door floats the hum of a spirit. When Suwelo asks her what she loves about the spirits that attract her, Fanny answers,

They open doors inside of me. It's as if they're keys. To rooms inside myself. I find a door inside and it's as if I hear a humming from behind it, and then I get inside somehow, with the key the old ones give me, and are, and as I stumble about in the darkness of the room, I begin to feel the stirring in myself, the humming of the room, and my heart starts to expand with the absolute feeling of bravery, or love, or audacity, or commitment. It becomes a light, and the light enters me, by osmosis, and a part of me that was not clear before is clarified. I radiate this expanded light. Happiness.
And *that*, Suwelo knew, was called "being in love." (*Temple*, 186)

When Fanny and Suwelo make love, he's never quite sure who is there. "I'm certainly not, as far as she's concerned, though she claims otherwise" (*Temple*, 185). Fanny's distractedness helps him to justify himself when he is unfaithful.

Neither Fanny's spirituality nor the hum of a spirit behind the closed door of her soul is difficult to understand considering her years in the home she shared with Celie and Shug after Celie's daughter, Olivia, surrendered to them her daughter's upbringing. By the time Fanny was a young child, Shug had founded her own church, complete with its *Gospel According to Shug* and its two-week "meetings" six times each year. All that this ill-assorted band of worshipers had in common was their belief that whatever they worshiped, whether it be trees or the air or the divinity that infuses all living beings, it had no name, a fact that made communicating about whatever "it" was difficult. Olivia explained to Celie and Shug that in Africa, the Olinka used humming instead of words for a concept that was fundamentally inexpressible. "Then the listener gets to interpret the hum, out of his own experience, and to know that there is a commonality of understanding possible but that true comprehension will always be a matter of degree. . . . So that is how they resolved it. They would hum the place G-O-D would occupy. Everyone in the house talked about *ummm* a lot!" (*Temple,* 170).

Suwelo describes Fanny as a "space cadet," but the relevant contrast between Miss Lissie and Fanny is not lost on him. He tells Miss Lissie, "You are a spirit that has had many bodies, and you travel through time and space that way. . . . Fanny is a body with many spirits shooting off to different realms every day" (*Temple,* 243).

Fanny wants her union with another physical being still to be an affair of the spirit. In frustration Suwelo one day asks Fanny why she loves him, if she indeed loves him at all, and she responds, "I love you for your breath." Suwelo thinks,

Typically, the least substantial thing about me! . . . Something unseen, indeed, invisible. Not my brains, not my cock, not my heart—no, my breath. But to her, as she explained it to me, my breath represented not only my life, but also the life force itself; and what this boiled down to in day-to-day reality is that she could, and did, kiss me all the time. We kissed for hours. Hours. She'd hold my tongue in her mouth and, with a shiver of pleasure that unfailingly caused me to rise almost beyond the occasion, she'd draw in my breath. Her own breath, sweet, delicious, the very essence of her soul's vitality, would enter me. (*Temple,* 283)

Miss Lissie and Hal laugh at his description, for they have known just such a union.

Fanny defines marriage as a bonding of souls so complete anyway that nothing a preacher could say about man's putting it asunder has any relevance and the marriage ceremony becomes a hypocrisy performed for the sake of the state. Divorce for Suwelo and Fanny thus means only "the first shedding of any nonintrinsic relatedness." Fanny moves out of their bedroom and eventually out of their house. Like their distant African ancestors, however, Fanny and Suwelo find that separate spaces increase their harmony rather than disrupt it. When they can come together as though meeting for the first time, their lovemaking has a freshness to it.

There is a security for Fanny in keeping her relationships as much as possible on a spiritual level, but hers is a false sense of security she knows she must overcome. At one point in the novel, as she gives Carlotta a massage, Fanny explains that she left academia to become a masseuse because she needed to touch the bodies of other people, even people she might not like, in order to force herself to confront their bodily reality and also their pain. "Otherwise," she says, "I am afraid I might start murdering them" (*Temple,* 293). Carlotta, who is about to begin an affair with Fanny's husband, feels her naked body stiffen under Fanny's usually soothing hands at the mention of murder, yet Fanny's anger is not that individualized, nor is it directed toward people of color.

Suwelo describes Fanny as a victim of racism who sees racism everywhere she looks and whose characteristic response is thoughts of violence. She tells her therapist about the shining, gold-handled sword that is constantly not in her hand but in her look and about her visions of blond heads rolling into the gutter. Out of fear of the murderer who exists within her, Fanny withdraws as far as possible from human contact, preferring the safer company of her spirit lovers.

Fanny takes a major step toward psychic health when she recognizes her anger for the fear that it really is. She does so with the help of her therapist, who uses hypnosis to get to the root of Fanny's feelings toward whites. Under hypnosis, Fanny admits that she envisions whites as always eating.

"Why do you feel afraid?"

"When I see them eating, I feel myself to be very hungry. Skin and bones. And I feel their teeth on my leg. But when I look down, sometimes it is not their teeth on my leg, only a cold chain. I am relieved to see it is not their teeth, only a chain. I think that when they called us 'cannibals' they were projecting."

"But why are you so afraid? If it is only a chain that is on your leg, and not their teeth; it can be broken. It can be filed away."

"Sometimes I see myself joining them at the table and I am eating, eating, eating, too. And we are all bloated and fat. We have chins down to our sternums, our eyes are clamped shut with fat. But the self that I was is still there, too. Right by the table, smelling the food. And she's as poor, as emaciated, as ever. She and her babies. Nothing but eyes and skin and bone. And

I am afraid, because I love her so very much, and she is the self I have lost. And the eating goes nowhere. It is endless gluttony to no purpose whatsoever. And I am afraid because aren't those *my* teeth on her leg?" (*Temple,* 314)

Fanny's hope is that she can stop racial oppression before it starts in her. "I won't be a racist," she tells her therapist. "I won't be a murderer. I won't do to them what they've done to black people. I'll die first" (*Temple,* 300).

Fanny's mother, Olivia, whose answer to what whites have done to blacks is forgiveness, whisks the agitated Fanny off to Africa to meet the father that she has never known. The father, Ola, knows what it is to take white lives—he has done so in the name of revolution—so he knows firsthand that killing the oppressors does not free one psychologically. His advice to his daughter is, rather, to harmonize her own heart. He knows that she alone can find the means of doing that, and she does so when she is able no longer to deny the body but rather to let spirit and flesh come together in a mutually nourishing way.

Early in the novel Suwelo plans to treat Fanny to one of Arveyda's concerts because she listens to his music endlessly, moved by it to a state of ecstasy. At the last moment, she finds herself suddenly paralyzed with fear at the prospect of meeting in the flesh a man "who created the beauty that was so much what her soul hungered for it made her weep. . . . 'Isn't Arveyda old?' she asked hopefully. (He wasn't.) 'I'll wait until he dies, or until *I* do, and then . . . I will see him'" (*Temple,* 129).

Only at the novel's end, when she finally meets Arveyda, does Fanny understand her habit of falling in love with people whom she will never meet. She is giving him one of her famous massages when she looks down at his naked back and thinks, "Is this how people create gods, . . . She thinks she has always been walking just behind (oh, a hundred to a thousand years behind) the people she has found to love, and that she has been very careful that their backs were turned. What would she do if one of them turned around?" (*Temple,* 406). When Arveyda does turn around, aroused by the motion of her hands on his body, their union with one another is a perfect blend of flesh and spirit: "After they make love, reaching climax almost immediately, they lie cuddled together in sheer astonishment. 'My . . . *spirit,*' says Fanny, at last, her face against his chest. 'My . . . *flesh,*' says Arveyda, his lips against her hair" (*Temple,* 408).

Fanny has learned not to deny the flesh out of fear of what her anger might lead her to do, but rather to harmonize her own heart and thus to achieve through union of body and soul the psychological wholeness that killing her oppressors could never bring. Arveyda is a fitting partner for her in that he, like the born-again Suwelo, is one of those rare men capable of understanding women's pain.

In her 1989 interview with Donna Britt of the *Washington Post,* Walker explained that she spent the early stages of the writing of *Temple* searching for reasons why people would willingly give over their spirituality to sources outside themselves. The answer, when it came, confirmed her belief that "the real temple of the spirit is not a church or synagogue, but freedom" (Britt, B4). In order to achieve spiritual freedom, Suwelo and Fanny, Carlotta and Arveyda have to return to the lifestyle of their ancestors, a lifestyle in which neither sex seeks dominion over the other and thus one in which neither sex must surrender its spirituality to the other. Each couple chooses to live apart—and free—in order to live in harmony.

The scene that gives the novel its title is Walker's warning against betrayal of one's own wild, untamed spirit. In the scene, Miss Lissie tells Suwelo of a dream in which she shows him her temple. Rushing about under foot is her familiar—part bird, part fish, part reptile. So distracting is its slithering and skidding about that she entraps it under a clear glass bowl, which it breaks through to escape. When the glass bowl fails to contain the creature, she tries a heavier white one and then finally, as a last resort, a metal wash tub. With the power of a volcano, the familiar breaks through the tub and out into the open air. "It looked at me with pity as it passed. Then, using wings it had never used before, it flew away" (*Temple,* 120). Miss Lissie realizes that out of pride and distraction she has betrayed the beautiful little familiar that had always been so loyal to her. She has betrayed her own spirit by trying to deny it the freedom of the cosmos.

Critical Discord

Walker's career has been in part a reaching back in time to retrieve the life and literary models that she felt were denied her. Throughout her works she has celebrated each link that has been forged between her and those who have gone before. *The Temple of My Familiar* carries that search to its limit. Asked by Oprah Winfrey in 1989 where the novel came from, Walker responded that it came "from me wanting to know my mama, you know. I wanted to know the very first woman, our common mother from all those years ago, and I just . . . thought and dreamed my way back to her."[1]

The reviews of *Temple of My Familiar* indicate that critics like their characters a bit more particularized in time and space. They also tend to favor a clash between characters as intrinsically more dramatic than a clash of ideas, and *Temple* proves once again that Walker's work is least successful as fiction when it is most polemical. When she began to rewrite the history of the world to accommodate her own racial and sexual chauvinism, reviewers wasted no time in making glib remarks about how many of her arboreal brothers and sisters gave their lives in order that the 416-page book might see print.

Chapter Ten
A Promise of Our Return at the End

When Walker early discovered that critics tended to focus more on Zora Neale Hurston's lifestyle than on her literary style, she nevertheless made the conscious decision that becoming a writer was worth the risk of critical disapprobation. A poem entitled "On Stripping Bark from Myself" that first appeared in *The American Poetry Review* in 1977 echoes the declaration of independence that she first made in a 1973 interview with John O'Brien. She declares that she will no longer live for what others believe, but rather will take her own stand against the world.[1]

The Alice Walker of the 1980s and early 1990s comes across as a woman at peace with herself. She has spent half a literary lifetime tracing women's search for self, including her own. Ironically, her harshest critics have focused on her portrayal not of women, but of men. One regret that she has is that such criticism merely succeeds once more in drawing attention away from injustices done to women. Another is that people tend to see only the negative behavior of her male characters.

Walker told Oprah Winfrey in 1989, "Why is it that they only see, they can only identify the negative behavior? . . . I think it's because it's the negative behavior, the macho behavior, that they see as male behavior and that when the men stop using that behavior, when the men become gentle, when the men become people you can talk to, when they are good grandparents, when they are gentle people, they are no longer considered men and there is an inability even to see them" (*Winfrey*). Critics often don't "see," or at least don't remember, that near the end of *The Color Purple,* a reformed Albert asks Celie to marry him again, this time in spirit as well as flesh. They forget that Grange Copeland comes back from his "second life" in New York a new and responsible man—and a loving grandfather. Truman Held takes on the burden that Meridian finally puts down when she walks away, refusing to be a martyr. And Suwelo in *Temple of My Familiar* grows from using

Carlotta's body without considering her pain to recognizing that she is far more than blind flesh, that indeed all women are. At the end of the novel, he has left university teaching and is learning carpentry, although he suffers pangs of guilt over the requisite slaughter of trees.

Walker already saw a "new man" beginning in some of her poetry from the 1970s. At first, she thought that new man would be one who, like Christ, put love in front and the necessary clenched fist behind, as she explains in "The Abduction of Saints." However, by the time she wrote the dedication to the 1984 volume that contains this poem, *Good Night, Willie Lee, I'll See You in the Morning,* she had set a slightly different standard for the new man. Her ideal man's rebellion now takes a more subtle form; he doesn't need fists. She calls him simply "the quiet man." Walker considers such a new, nurturing man essential for the survival of the planet.

If nothing else could have moved Walker to put aside the anger so characteristic of her early years, her concern for her planet has done so. She told Winfrey in the same interview, "There is no heaven. This is it. We're already in heaven, you know, and so in order . . . for the earth to survive, we have to acknowledge each other as part of the family, the same family, and also reaffirm those things in ourselves and in other people that we've been brought up to fear or to hate" (*Winfrey*).

Walker acknowledges and prays to a Great Spirit that sounds suspiciously like God without the male trappings formerly incompatible with her womanist sensibilities. In the last essay in *Living by the Word,* "The Universe Responds," written in 1987, she defines prayer as "the active affirmation in the physical world of our inseparableness from the divine" (*Living,* 192), and she ends with this adaptation of the Gospels:

Knock and the door shall be opened. Ask and you shall receive.

Whatsoever you do unto the least of these, you do also unto me—and to yourself. For we are one.

"God" answers prayers. Which is another way of saying, "the Universe responds."

We are *indeed* the world. Only if we have reason to fear what is in our own hearts need we fear for the planet. Teach yourself peace.

Pass it on. (*Living,* 193)

In the title poem of *Good Night, Willie Lee, I'll See You in the Morning,* Walker's mother says good-bye to her husband at his death with words that quietly assume their parting is not permanent. When Walker heard those words, she recognized the healing power of forgiveness that promises that there will indeed be a final return in the end.

In her 31 August 1984 journal entry Walker wrote to her Great Spirit, "There is no doubt in my mind that I am blessed. That you are present in the cosmos and in me and that we are breathing together—conspiracy. I see now what is meant by faith and the giving up of the self to the spirit. I thank you for your gifts. All of them. I see you are trying to teach me all the time. I think of this when the lessons hurt" (*Living,* 52–53). The new woman that Walker has become has learned not to confront the world with a clenched fist—although like her version of Christ she may simply hide it behind her back most of the time—but rather with the open hand of unity.

Notes and References

Preface

1. Alice Walker, *Living by the Word: Selected Writings 1973–1987* (San Diego: Harcourt Brace Jovanovich, 1988), 95; hereinafter cited in text as *Living*.

Chapter One

1. Alice Walker, *In Search of Our Mothers' Gardens: Womanist Prose* (San Diego: Harcourt Brace Jovanovich, 1983), 260; hereinafter cited in text as *Gardens*.
2. Alice Walker, *The Third Life of Grange Copeland* (San Diego: Harcourt Brace Jovanovich, 1970); hereinafter cited in text as *Copeland*.
3. Alice Walker, *Revolutionary Petunias and Other Poems* (San Diego: Harcourt Brace Jovanovich, 1973), 6; hereinafter cited in text as *Petunias*. Permission to quote from Walker's poetry was denied.
4. "From an Interview" is reprinted from John O'Brien, *Interviews with Black Writers* (New York: Liveright, 1973), 185–211; hereinafter cited in text.
5. Mary Helen Washington, "Alice Walker: Her Mother's Gifts," *Ms.*, June 1982, 38; hereinafter cited in text.
6. David Bradley, "Telling the Black Woman's Story," *New York Times Magazine,* 8 January 1984, 36; hereinafter cited in text.
7. "Afterword," *The Third Life of Grange Copeland* (New York: Pocket Books, 1988), 344; hereinafter cited in text as "Afterword."
8. Gregory Jaynes, "Living by the Word," *Life,* May 1989, 62; hereinafter cited in text.
9. Alice Walker, *You Can't Keep a Good Woman Down* (San Diego: Harcourt Brace Jovanovich, 1981), 124–37; hereinafter cited in text as *GW*.
10. Alice Walker, *Once: Poems* (San Diego: Harcourt Brace Jovanovich, 1976); hereinafter cited in text.
11. Alice Walker, *In Love and Trouble: Stories of Black Women* (San Diego: Harcourt Brace Jovanovich, 1973), 129–38; hereinafter cited in text as *Trouble.*
12. Alice Walker, *To Hell with Dying* (San Diego: Harcourt Brace Jovanovich, 1988).
13. Alice Walker, "To Hell with Dying," in *Best Short Stories by Negro Writers: An Anthology from 1899 to the Present,* ed. Langston Hughes (Boston: Little, Brown, 1967), 490–96.

14. Alice Walker, *Langston Hughes: American Poet* (New York: Crowell, 1974).

Chapter Two

1. Alice Walker, ed., *I Love Myself When I Am Laughing . . . And Then Again When I Am Looking Mean and Impressive: A Zora Neale Hurston Reader* (Old Westbury, N. Y.: Feminist Press, 1979).
2. Donna Britt, "Alice Walker and the Inner Mysteries Unraveled," *Washington Post,* 8 May 1989, B1, B4.
3. Alice Walker, *Meridian* (New York: Washington Square Press, 1976); hereinafter cited in text.
4. Alice Walker, *The Color Purple* (New York: Pocket Books, 1982); hereinafter cited in text as *Purple.*
5. Alice Walker, *Temple of My Familiar* (San Diego: Harcourt Brace Jovanovich, 1989); hereinafter cited in text as *Temple.*

Chapter Three

1. Barbara Christian, "Contrary Women of Alice Walker: A Study of Female Protagonists in *In Love and Trouble* (1980)," in *Black Feminist Criticism: Perspectives on Black Women Writers* (New York: Pergamon Press, 1985), 38.
2. In an interview with Claudia Tate, published as "Alice Walker," in *Black Women Writers at Work* (New York: Continuum, 1983), Walker stated, "I wrote 'The Child Who Favored Daughter' in 1966, after my first summer in Mississippi. I wrote it out of trying to understand how a black father would feel about a daughter who fell in love with a white man. Now, this was very apropos because I had just come out of a long engagement with a young man who was white, and my father never accepted him. I did not take his nonacceptance lightly. I knew I needed to understand the depth of his antagonism. After all, I was 20 or so, and couldn't quite understand his feelings since history is taught in the slapdash fashion that it is taught. I needed to comprehend what was going on with him and what would go on with any black man of his generation brought up in the South, having children in the South, whose child fell in love with someone who is 'the enemy.'

"I had been writing the story for, oh I guess, almost six months and I took it with me to Mississippi. Ironically, it was over that story, in a sense, that I met the man I did, in fact, marry. We met in the movement in Mississippi, and I was dragging around this notebook, saying, 'I'm a writer.' Most people think when you say you're a writer, and especially when you're twenty, that you can't be serious. Well, I read the story to him and he was convinced" (186–87).

Chapter Four

   1. Trudier Harris, "Three Black Women Writers and Humanism: A Folk Perspective," in *Black American Literature and Humanism,* ed. R. Baxter Miller (Lexington: University Press of Kentucky, 1981), 58–65.
   2. W. Lawrence Hogue, "History, the Feminist Discourse, and Alice Walker's *The Third Life of Grange Copeland,*" *MELUS* 12 (1972): 49–50.
   3. Mary Helen Washington, "An Essay on Alice Walker," in *Sturdy Black Bridges: Visions of Black Women in Literature,* ed. Roseann P. Bell et al. (Garden City, N. Y.: Anchor Press/Doubleday, 1979), 133–56.
   4. Klaus Ensslen, "Collective Experience and Individual Responsibility: Alice Walker's *The Third Life of Grange Copeland,*" in *The Afro-American Novel since 1960,* ed. Peter Bruck and Wolfgang Karrer (Amsterdam: B. R. Gruner, 1982), 199–200.
   5. In the 1988 afterword to the Pocket Books edition, Walker explains that Mem's death was based on a real case in her hometown of Eatonton, Georgia. The mother of one of Walker's classmates, also named Walker, was shot in the face by her husband, and Walker saw the body when her own sister, a beautician and cosmetologist who worked for the funeral home, invited her into the room where the victim lay. Walker writes, "I describe her in the novel exactly as she appeared to me then. Writing about it years later was the only way I could be free of such a powerful and despairing image. . . . Seeing the body of Mrs. Walker there on the enamel table, I realized that indeed, she might have been my own mother and that perhaps in relation to men she was also symbolic of all women, not only including my husband's grandmother and mother, who were as different from my own, I had thought, as possible, but also of me. That is why she is named Mem, in the novel, after the French *la meme,* meaning 'the same'" (343–44).

Chapter Five

   1. Rudolph P. Byrd, in "Spirituality in the Novels of Alice Walker: Models, Healing, and Transformation, or When the Spirit Moves So Do We," in *Wild Women in the Whirlwind: Afra-American Culture and the Contemporary Literary Renaissance,* ed. Joanne M. Braxton and Andree N. McLaughlin (New Brunswick, N. J.: Rutgers University Press, 1990), provides some interesting background on the name Meridian Hill: "As we know, Meridian Hill is the name of the heroine in Walker's novel, but there is also a beautiful spot in northwest Washington, D.C., called Meridian Hill Park, a park often visited by a young Jean Toomer. Built in 1910 from a design by Horace C. Peaslee, Meridian Hill Park is an approximation of a formal Italian garden. Toomer, who as a boy lived within walking distance of the park, was doubtless drawn there by its splendid vista. On this bluff he could see, with one glance, the

White House, the Washington Monument, the Potomac River, and the hills of Virginia. Meridian Hill Park was a special place for Toomer because it was here that he—inspired by the vista, the scowl worn by the towering monument to Dante, and the romantic representation of Joan of Arc—dreamed of becoming a poet. But Meridian Hill Park, as Walker surely knows, is not without geographic and astronomical significance. It was here in 1816 that the "meridian was surveyed in the vain hope of establishing a new prime meridian to free American navigators from dependence on that of Greenwich" [E. J. Applewhite, *Washington Itself* (New York: Alfred A. Knopf, 1981), 99]. Interestingly, by resolution of the District government Meridian Hill Park was renamed Malcolm X Park—a fact very much in keeping with the spirit of Walker's novel—a park where other young men, attracted by the formal garden and the view, pause to dream but not, so rumor has it, exclusively of poetry" (370).

2. Karen Stein, "*Meridian*: Alice Walker's Critique of Revolution," *Black American Literature Forum* 20 (Spring–Summer 1986): 129–30.

Chapter Six

1. Kay Bonetti, "An Interview with Alice Walker" (Columbia, MO.: American Audio Prose Library, 1981); hereinafter cited in the text.

Chapter Seven

1. Susan Dworkin, "The Making of *The Color Purple*," *Ms.*, December 1985, 68; hereinafter cited in text.

2. Sharon Wilson, "A Conversation with Alice Walker," *Kalliope* 6, no. 2 (1984): 38.

3. Mae Henderson, "*The Color Purple*: Revisions and Redefinitions," *SAGE* 2.1 (Spring 1985): 16.

4. Wendy Wall, "Lettered Bodies and Corporeal Texts in *The Color Purple*," *Studies in American Fiction* 16.1 (Spring 1988): 89; hereinafter cited in text.

5. Bernard W. Bell, *The Afro-American Novel and Its Traditions* (Amherst: University of Massachusetts Press, 1987), 263; hereinafter cited in text.

6. Ntozake Shange, *for colored girls who have considered suicide/when the rainbow is enuf* (New York: Bantam, 1975), 67.

Chapter Eight

1. Alice Walker, *Horses Make a Landscape Look More Beautiful* (San Diego: Harvest/HBJ, 1986), viii; hereinafter cited in text as *Horses*.

Chapter Nine

1. *Oprah Winfrey Show #710,* Harpo Productions, Inc., 2 June 1989; hereinafter cited in text as *Winfrey.*

Chapter Ten

1. Alice Walker, *Good Night, Willie Lee, I'll See You in the Morning* (San Diego: Harcourt Brace Jovanovich, 1984), 23; hereinafter cited in text as *Willie Lee.*

Selected Bibliography

PRIMARY SOURCES

Novels

The Color Purple. San Diego: Harcourt Brace Jovanovich, 1982. London: Womanist Press, 1983. New York: Washington Square Press, 1983. New York: Pocket Books, 1985.

Meridian. New York: Harcourt Brace Jovanovich, 1976. New York: Washington Square Press, 1977.

The Temple of My Familiar. San Diego: Harcourt Brace Jovanovich, 1989. New York: Pocket Books, 1990.

The Third Life of Grange Copeland. New York: Harcourt Brace Jovanovich, 1970. New York: Pocket Books, 1988.

Essays

In Search of Our Mothers' Gardens: Womanist Prose. San Diego: Harcourt Brace Jovanovich, 1983. San Diego: Harvest/HBJ, 1984.

Living by the Word: Selected Writings 1973–1987. San Diego: Harcourt Brace Jovanovich, 1988.

Short Stories

In Love and Trouble: Stories of Black Women. San Diego: Harvest/HBJ, 1973.

You Can't Keep a Good Woman Down. San Diego: Harvest/HBJ, 1981. London: Women's Press, 1982.

Poetry

Good Night, Willie Lee, I'll See You in the Morning: Poems. New York: Dial, 1979. San Diego: Harvest/HBJ, 1984.

Her Blue Body Everything We Know: Earthling Poems 1965–1990 Complete. San Diego: Harcourt Brace Jovanovich, 1991.

Horses Make a Landscape Look More Beautiful. San Diego: Harcourt Brace Jovanovich, 1984. San Diego: Harvest/HBJ, 1986.

Once: Poems. San Diego: Harcourt Brace Jovanovich, 1968. San Diego: Harvest/HBJ, 1976.

Revolutionary Petunias and Other Poems. San Diego: Harcourt Brace Jovanovich, 1973. San Diego: Harvest/HBJ, 1973.

Children's Books

Langston Hughes: American Poet. New York: Crowell, 1974.
To Hell with Dying. San Diego: Harcourt Brace Jovanovich, 1988.

Edited Work

I Love Myself When I Am Laughing . . . And Then Again When I Am Looking Mean and Impressive: A Zora Neale Hurston Reader. Old Westbury, N. Y.: Feminist Press, 1979.

SECONDARY SOURCES

Books and Parts of Books

Bell, Bernard W. "The Contemporary Afro-American Novel, 1: Neorealism." In *The Afro-American Novel and Its Tradition,* 259–69. Amherst: University of Massachusetts Press, 1987. "By exploring the oppressions and celebrating the triumphs of Southern black wives, mothers, and daughters as they relate more to each other than to working-class black men, [Walker] tailors the tradition of critical realism to fit into folk romance and reinforces the theme of black feminism in the Afro-American novel."

Bloom, Harold, ed. *Alice Walker.* New York: Chelsea House, 1989. A "representative selection of the best criticism available upon the writings of Alice Walker" through 1988. Ten of the thirteen essays are reprints from other sources; three are printed here for the first time.

Byerman, Keith E. "Women's Blues: The Fiction of Toni Cade Bambara and Alice Walker." In *Fingering the Jagged Grain: Tradition and Form in Recent Black Fiction,* 104–70. Athens: University of Georgia Press, 1985. Examines the clash in the fiction of Walker and Toni Cade Bambara between a folk culture that has survival as its objective and a feminist ideology that has political power as its objective.

Christian, Barbara. "Alice Walker: The Black Woman Artist as Wayward." In *Black Women Writers (1950–80): A Critical Evaluation,* edited by Mari Evans, 457–77. Garden City, N. Y.: Anchor Press/Doubleday, 1984. Reprinted in Christian, *Black Feminist Criticism,* 81–101. Looks at all of Walker's works through 1982 in the context of the time they were written and as part of Afro-American women's intellectual tradition.

————. "The Contrary Women of Alice Walker: A Study of Female Protagonists in *In Love and Trouble*." In *Black Feminist Criticism: Perspectives on Black Women Writers*, 31–46. New York: Pergamon Press, 1985. Analyzes the stories in *In Love and Trouble* in light of the pain and violence the female protagonists endure but also the contrariness that leads them to fight against forces that would deny them wholeness.

————. "No More Buried Lives: The Theme of Lesbianism in Audre Lourde's *Zami*, Gloria Naylor's *The Women of Brewster Place*, Ntozake Shange's *Sassafras, Cypress, and Indigo,* and Alice Walker's *The Color Purple*." In *Black Feminist Criticism: Perspectives on Black Women Writers*, 187–204. New York: Pergamon Press, 1985. Deals with the emergence of the theme of lesbianism in novels by black women in recent years. The four books she examines show the spectrum of lesbian experience.

————. "Novels for Everyday Use: The Novels of Alice Walker." In *Black Women Novelists: The Development of a Tradition, 1892–1976*, 180–238. Westport, Conn.: Greenwood, 1980. An excellent and detailed analysis of *The Third Life of Grange Copeland* and *Meridian* as illustrative of the conflict between the human spirit and societal patterns, revealing the process of "personal and social growth out of horror and waste."

Ensslen, Klaus. "Collective Experience and Individual Responsibility: Alice Walker's *The Third Life of Grange Copeland*." In *The Afro-American Novel since 1960*, edited by Peter Bruck and Wolfgang Karrer, 189–218. Amsterdam: B. R. Gruner, 1982. Examines how in *The Third Life of Grange Copeland* Walker uses Grange's adult life to dramatize the collective experience of rural Southern blacks as they move from economic and psychological dependence toward a self awareness that leads to revised self-concepts and the new social roles based on them.

Fontenot, Chester J. "Alice Walker: 'The Diary of an African Nun' and DuBois' Double Consciousness." In *Sturdy Black Bridges: Visions of Black Women in Literature*, edited by Roseann P. Bell et al., 150–56. Garden City, N. Y.: Anchor Press/Doubleday, 1979. Applies DuBois's theory that blacks in the United States feel a double consciousness of themselves as blacks and as Americans to main character of Walker's short story, who feels pulled between her African roots and the Christianity that calls her to reject them.

Gates, Henry Louis, Jr. "Color Me Zora: Alice Walker's (Re)Writing of the Speakerly Text." In *The Signifying Monkey: A Theory of Afro-American Criticism*, 239–58. New York: Oxford University Press, 1988. Analyzes *The Color Purple* as Walker's rewriting of Hurston's narrative strategy. The chapter, as part of Gates's exploration of the relation between black vernacular tradition and the Afro-American literary tradition, is somewhat difficult to comprehend when not read in the context of the whole work.

Harris, Trudier. "Three Black Women Writers and Humanism: A Folk Perspective." In *Black American Literature and Humanism*, edited by R. Baxter Miller, 58–65. Lexington: University Press of Kentucky, 1981. Explores the rejection of Christianity "in favor of a more exacting and humanistic idealism" by Walker's Grange Copeland, Paule Marshall's Merle Kimbona, and Sarah E. Wright's Mariah Upshur.

Hite, Molly. "Romance, Marginality, Matrilineage: *The Color Purple.*" In *The Other Side of the Story: Structures and Strategies of Contemporary Feminist Narrative*, 103–26. Ithaca, N. Y.: Cornell University Press, 1989. Hite finds those who read *The Color Purple* as a realistic novel guilty of the intentional fallacy. She analyzes the novel, rather, as a Shakespearean romance.

McDowell, Deborah E. "Reading Family Matters." In *Changing Our Own Words: Essays on Criticism, Theory, and Writing by Black Women*, edited by Cheryl A. Wall, 75–97. New Brunswick, N. J.: Rutgers University Press, 1989. Most extensive analysis of "Source" available. Perceives the story as a narrative about conflicting discourses about family and identity.

Mickelson, Anne Z. *Reaching Out: Sensitivity and Order in Recent Fiction by Women*, 112–74. Metuchen, N. J.: Scarecrow Press, 1979. Analyzes love, marriage, and the female characters' search for dignity in *In Love and Trouble* and Meridian Hill's search for independence in *Meridian*.

O'Brien, John. "Alice Walker." In *Interviews with Black Writers*, 185–211. New York: Liveright, 1973. An extremely important work because it records Walker speaking very candidly about her life and her early works. This is the source to which many later researchers into Walker's life and art have turned as a starting point. Some of the major themes of all her works are introduced here.

Parker-Smith, Bettye J. "Alice Walker's Women: In Search of Some Peace of Mind." In *Black Women Writers (1950–80): A Critical Evaluation*, edited by Mari Evans, 478–93. Garden City, N. Y.: Anchor Press/Doubleday, 1984. Traces the evolution of Walker's female characters from the powerlessness of pain and suffering to the triumph of self-love.

Pullin, Faith. "Landscapes of Reality: The Fiction of Contemporary Afro-American Women." In *Black Fiction: New Studies in the Afro-American Novel since 1945*, edited by A. Robert Lee, 173–203. New York: Barnes and Noble, 1980. A useful analysis of stories from *In Love and Trouble*.

Spillers, Hortense J. "'The Permanent Obliquity of an In(pha)llibly Straight': In the Time of Daughters and Fathers." In *Changing Our Own Words: Essays on Criticism, Theory, and Writing by Black Women*, edited by Cheryl A. Wall, 127–49. New Brunswick, N. J.: Rutgers University Press, 1989. An analysis of the theme of incest in Walker's "The Child Who Favored Daughter" and Ellison's *Invisible Man*, obscured somewhat by Spillers's idiosyncratic style.

Tate, Claudia. "Alice Walker." In *Black Women Writers at Work*, 175–87. New York: Continuum, 1983. A late 1979 or early 1980 interview in which

Walker candidly discusses her intentions as a writer and some of the history behind her early works.

Wade-Gayles, Gloria. "Giving Birth to Self: The Quests for Wholeness of Sula Mae Peace and Meridian Hill." In *No Crystal Stair: Visions of Race and Sex in Black Women's Fiction,* 184–215. New York: Pilgrim Press, 1984. Describes these two characters as having in common the intense desire to give birth to themselves as persons, women who will not be restricted to narrow definitions of themselves as women.

————. "The Halo and the Hardships: Black Women as Mothers and Sometimes as Wives." In *No Crystal Stair: Visions of Race and Sex in Black Women's Fiction,* 57–113. New York: Pilgrim Press, 1984. Looks at the myth of the "sacred calling" of motherhood and the tension between that myth and the reality of motherhood as experienced by Mrs. Hill in *Meridian,* Pauline Breedlove in *The Bluest Eye,* Eva Peace in *Sula,* and Mem Copeland in *The Third Life of Grange Copeland.*

Washington, Mary Helen. "An Essay on Alice Walker." In *Sturdy Black Bridges: Visions of Black Women in Literature,* edited by Roseann P. Bell et al., 133–49. Garden City, N. Y.: Anchor Press/Doubleday, 1979. An overview of Walker as apologist and spokeswoman for black women particularly useful in its discussion of the cycles through which Walker's women had progressed in her works through *Meridian.*

————. "I Sign My Mother's Name: Alice Walker, Dorothy West, Paule Marshall." In *Mothering the Mind: Twelve Studies of Writers and Their Silent Partners,* edited by Ruth Perry and Martine Watson Brownley, 143–63. New York: Holmes and Meier, 1984. Washington applied to Walker, West, and Marshall and their relationships with their mothers her belief that "as either conscious myth or literal reality, the connection between the mother and daughter and the daughter's decision to be a writer are essentially interrelated." Discusses how her mother's history influenced Walker's writing of "The Revenge of Hannah Kemhuff."

Willis, Susan. "Alice Walker's Women." In *Specifying: Black Women Writing the American Experience,* 110–28. Madison: University of Wisconsin Press, 1987. Explores the themes of return as developmental imperative and of relationship to the group as political paradigm in Walker's novels.

Articles

Babb, Valerie. "*The Color Purple*: Writing to Undo What Writing Has Done." *Phylon* 47 (Summer 1986): 107–16. Argues that in *The Color Purple* Walker reorganizes the hierarchy that gives whites power over blacks, men power over women, and written expression power over oral expression.

Bobo, Jacqueline. "Sifting through the Controversy: Reading *The Color Pur-*

ple." Callaloo 12, no. 2 (1989): 332–42. A useful summary of the controversy spawned by both the novel and the film.

Bradley, David. "Telling the Black Woman's Story." *New York Times Magazine,* 8 January 1984, 24–37. A black male writer's reflections on his reading of and conversations with Walker.

Britt, Donna. "Alice Walker and the Inner Mysteries Unraveled." *Washington Post,* 8 May 1989, B1, B4. Based on an interview with Walker when *Temple of My Familiar* was published, provides background on the writing of the novel and on Walker's response to the reception of her earlier works.

Buncombe, Marie H. "Androgyny as Metaphor in Alice Walker's Novels." *CLA Journal* 30 (June 1987): 419–27. Contends that in her novels Walker uses androgyny as a metaphor for wholeness.

Byerman, Keith. "Desire and Alice Walker: The Quest for a Womanist Narrative." *Callaloo* 12 (Spring 1989): 321–31. A Lacanian look at three pieces from *You Can't Keep a Good Woman Down*: "Coming Apart," "Porn," and "Advancing Luna—and Ida B. Wells."

Byrd, Rudolph P. "Sound Advice from a Friend: Words and Thoughts on the Higher Ground of Alice Walker." *Callaloo* 6 (Spring–Summer 1983): 123–29. A good overview of *In Search of Our Mothers' Gardens,* which calls the collection "splendid" and declares it the first essay collection produced by a black female writer yet which allots a disproportionate amount of space to trying to prove that Jean Toomer did not attempt to pass for white as Walker claims.

Callahan, John. "The Higher Ground of Alice Walker." *New Republic,* 14 September 1974, 21–22. Review of *Once, Grange Copeland, Revolutionary Petunias,* and *In Love and Trouble.*

Cheung, King-Kok. "'Don't Tell': Imposed Silences in *The Color Purple* and *The Woman Warrior." PMLA* 103 (March 1988): 162–74. An excellent discussion of Walker's *The Color Purple* and Maxine Hong Kingston's *Woman Warrior,* in which "breaking silence, acknowledging female influence, and preserving cultural and national characteristics are a coordinated art."

Davis, Jane. "*The Color Purple*: A Spiritual Descendent of Hurston's *Their Eyes Were Watching God." Griot* 6 (Summer 1987): 79–96. A poorly edited but insightful comparison of Hurston's novel and Walker's.

Davis, Thadious M. "Alice Walker's Celebration of Self in Southern Generations." *Southern Quarterly* 21 (Summer 1983): 38–53. Draws examples from Walker's essays, short stories, and novels to illustrate how Walker has used patterns of generations to portray who her people are and what their lives mean.

Dworkin, Susan. "The Strange and Wonderful Story of the Making of *The Color Purple." Ms.,* December 1985, 66–70, 94–95. A behind-the-scenes look at Walker's role in the production of the movie version of *The Color Purple*.

Erickson, Peter. "'Cast Out Alone/To Heal/And Re-create//Ourselves': Family-Based Identity in the Work of Alice Walker." *CLA Journal*, 23 (Spring 1979): 71–94. An excellent discussion of Walker's exploration of intrafamily relationships in *The Third Life of Grange Copeland*, "A Sudden Trip Home in the Spring," *Meridian*, and *Revolutionary Petunias*.

Gaston, Karen C. "Women in the Lives of Grange Copeland." *CLA Journal* 24, no. 3 (1981): 276–86. A clear analysis of the central role of the women in *The Third Life of Grange Copeland*.

Gernes, Sonia. Review of *Horses Make a Landscape Look More Beautiful*. *America*, 2 February 1985, 93–94. A brief, well-written, and generally positive review, emphasizing the collection as Walker's ruminations on the effects of heritage.

Hairston, Loyle. "Alice in the Mainstream." *Freedomways* 24 (Summer 1984): 182–90. In this essay review of *In Search of Our Mothers' Gardens*, Hairston praises Walker as an artist yet argues that she has been welcomed into the literary mainstream because "there is little in her fictional world luminous enough to cast damaging light on the socio-economic vice in which Afro-Americans and other third world peoples find themselves in U. S. society."

Harris, Trudier. "From Victimization to Free Enterprise: Alice Walker's *The Color Purple*." *Studies in American Fiction* 14 (Spring 1986): 1–17. Argues that the progression in Walker's world from male control of females' lives to the women's control of their own lives culminates in the character of Celie, but that the change comes at the expense of realistic portrayals of black female characters.

————. "On *The Color Purple*, Stereotypes, and Silence." *Black American Literature Forum* 18 (Winter 1984): 155–61. An excellent analysis of the uncomfortable position black women critics are placed in criticizing *The Color Purple*. Details the weaknesses of the novel.

————. "Tiptoeing through Taboo: Incest in 'The Child Who Favored Daughter.'" *Modern Fiction Studies* 28, no. 3 (1982): 495–505. Points out that incest has been among those subjects particularly taboo to black American writers, but traces the history of the breaking of that taboo, focusing on incest in "The Child Who Favored Daughter."

————. "Folklore in the Fiction of Alice Walker: A Perpetuation of Historical and Literary Traditions." *Black American Literature Forum* 11 (1977): 3–8. Explores Walker's use of folklore as a means of character and plot development in "The Revenge of Hannah Kemhuff" and "Everday Use."

Hellenbrand, Harold. "Speech, After Silence: Alice Walker's *The Third Life of Grange Copeland*." *Black American Literature Forum* 20 (Spring–Summer 1986): 113–28. Traces how Grange Copeland's "murder" of a white woman in his "second life" moves him from the silence of his first to the storytelling of his third.

Henderson, Mae G. "*The Color Purple*: Revisions and Redefinitions." *SAGE* 2, no. 1 (1985): 14–18. Illustrates how *The Color Purple* reverses some of the codes and conventions of the epistolary novel and how those reversals symbolize the subversion of the codes and conventions which dominate social and sexual relationships.

Hogue, W. Lawrence. "History, the Feminist Discourse, and Alice Walker's *The Third Life of Grange Copeland*." *MELUS* 12 (Summer 1985): 45–62. This unfortunately jargon-ridden article uses Foucault's concept of discourse formation to explain how social discourse informs literary texts.

Hollister, Michael. "Tradition in Alice Walker's 'To Hell with Dying.'" *Studies in Short Fiction* 26 (Winter 1989): 90–94. A detailed analysis of "To Hell with Dying" that traces its emotional power to universalist values, archetypal imagery, and recurrent rhythms.

Jaynes, Gregory. "Living by the Word," *Life,* May 1989, 62. Jaynes interviewed Walker when *Temple of My Familiar* was published and here recaps her life and accomplishments to that point, noting how the angry Walker has mellowed with time.

Kennedy, Randall. "Looking for Zora." Review of *I Love Myself When I Am Laughing. New York Times Book Review,* 30 December 1979, 8, 17. Argues that Walker's Hurston reader does more than redress an injustice of literary history by making some of Hurston's works available. It also reflects significant trends in Afro-American culture such as the emergence of self-conscious feminism, increasing sophistication in the study of black literature, and a renewed emphasis on black nationalism.

Lupton, Mary Jane. "Clothes and Closure in Three Novels by Black Women." *Black American Literature Forum* 20 (Winter 1986): 409–21. Reads Walker's *The Color Purple,* Jessie Fauset's *Comedy: American Style,* and Toni Morrison's *Tar Baby* in light of the Cinderella myth and the use of clothing as a sign of character, gender, and race and as a vehicle for transformation of the self.

McDowell, Deborah E. "'The Changing Same': Generational Connections and Black Women Novelists." *New Literary History* 18 (Winter 1987): 281–302. Uses Frances E. W. Harper's *Iola Leroy* and *The Color Purple* to illustrate public and private narrative fiction.

———. "The Self in Bloom: Alice Walker's *Meridian*." *CLA Journal* 24 (March 1981): 262–75. Excellent discussion of *Meridian* as *bildungsroman*.

Smith, Valerie. "Creating Connections." Review of *In Search of Our Mothers' Gardens. Sewanee Review* 93 (Spring 1985): xxxi–xxxiv. A positive review that states the collected essays "offer a subtle and compelling portrait of the author's mind and display the versatility of her talent," focusing on the value of continuity.

Stein, Karen F. "*Meridian*: Alice Walker's Critique of Revolution." *Black American Literature Forum* 20 (Spring–Summer 1986): 129–41. Analyzes Walker's reappraisal of the civil rights movement in light of her evolving commitment to feminism, using *Meridian* to illustrate the change.

Tavormina, M. Teresa. "Dressing the Spirit: Clothworking and Language in *The Color Purple*." *Journal of Narrative Technique* 16 (Fall 1986): 220–30. An intriguing account of the thematically related roles of clothing and language in *The Color Purple*.

Walker, Robbie. "Coping Strategies of the Women in Alice Walker's Novels: Implications for Survival." *CLA Journal* 30 (June 1987): 401–18. Contrasts the coping strategies of three Walker women who have in common humble beginnings and lives characterized by brutality and hopelessness: Margaret and Mem from *Grange Copeland* and Celie from *The Color Purple*.

Wall, Wendy. "Lettered Bodies and Corporeal Texts in *The Color Purple*." *Studies in American Fiction* 16 (Spring 1988): 83–97. Excellent analysis of how Celie first submits to forces of authority that imprint themselves physically on her body yet later discovers through her letters a "second body" that allows her to define herself against the patriarchy.

Walsh, Margaret. "The Enchanted World of *The Color Purple*." *Southern Quarterly* 25 (Winter 1987): 89–101. A reading of *The Color Purple* as fairy tale.

Washington, Mary Helen. "Alice Walker: Her Mother's Gifts." *Ms.*, June 1982, 38. Reports on a discussion Washington had with Walker about the gifts, spiritual and literal, that came to Walker from her mother, empowering her to write.

Weston, Ruth D. "Inversion of Patriarchal Mantle Images in Alice Walker's *Meridian*." *Southern Quarterly* 25 (Winter 1987): 102–107. An interesting analysis of Walker's use of reversal of the biblical mantle image in terms of the patriarch as protector.

Williams, Mary C. "The Poetic Knife: Poetry by Recent Southern Women Poets." *South Carolina Review* 11 (November 1978): 44–59. Brief treatment of Walker's *Once* and *Revolutionary Petunias* in the context of an analysis of poetry by recent Southern women poets.

Williamson, Alan. "In a Middle Style." *Poetry* 135 (March 1980): 348–54. This essay review briefly treats both the strengths and the weaknesses of *Good Night, Willie Lee, I'll See You in the Morning*.

Wilson, Sharon. "A Conversation with Alice Walker." *Kalliope* 6, no. 2 (1984): 37–45. Transcript of an interview conducted as part of the "Worth Quoting" series in Jacksonville, Florida.

Winchell, Mark Royden. "Fetching the Doctor: Shamanistic Housecalls in Alice Walker's 'Strong Horse Tea.'" *Mississippi Folklore Register* 15 (Fall 1981): 97–101. An analysis of Walker's use of folk medicine in "Strong Horse Tea."

Audiotape

Bonetti, Kay. "An Interview with Alice Walker." Columbia, Mo.: American Audio Prose Library, 1981.

Telecast

The Oprah Winfrey Show #710, Harpo Productions, 2 June 1989.

Bibliographies

Banks, Erma Davis, and Keith Byerman. *Alice Walker: An Annotated Bibliography 1968–86.* New York: Garland, 1989. An extremely useful volume that opens with a 20-page introduction to biography, works and response, and literary criticism, then provides one thousand citations, including primary works, general book criticism and reference sources, general periodical sources and interviews, criticism of individual works, and bibliographies. Entries on all secondary sources are annotated.

Byerman, Keith, and Erma Banks. "Alice Walker: A Selected Bibliography, 1968–88." *Callaloo* 12, no. 2 (1989): 343–45. Very limited, but does include a few entries too recent to have been included in Banks and Byerman's 1989 Garland bibliography.

Kirschner, Susan. "Alice Walker's Nonfictional Prose: A Checklist, 1966–1984." *Black American Literature Forum* 18 (Winter 1984): 162–63. Useful as a means of locating works uncollected as of 1984 and of locating where works in *Gardens* originally appeared.

Pratt, Louis H., and Darnell D. Pratt. *Alice Malsenior Walker: An Annotated Bibliography: 1968–1986.* Westport: Meckler, 1988. A useful work that includes 420 secondary sources with descriptive annotations, in addition to a listing of primary works up to 1986 and an introduction.

Index

The Author

Donna Haisty Winchell holds B. A. and M. A. degrees from Florida State University and the Ph.D. from Texas Christian University. She is currently an associate professor of English at Clemson University, where she teaches composition, composition theory, and ethnic American literature. Her developmental English text, *Writer, Audience, Subject: Bridging the Communication Gap,* with Mary Sue Ply, was published by Scott, Foresman in 1989, and she has published on developmental psychology and basic writers in *Research in Basic Writing: A Bibliographic Sourcebook.*

The Editor

Frank Day is a professor of English at Clemson University. He is the author of *Sir William Empson: An Annotated Bibliography* and *Arthur Koestler: A Guide to Research*. He was a Fulbright Lecturer in American Literature in Romania (1980–81) and in Bangladesh (1986–87).